Nev Ghosted Again

15 Reasons Why Men Lose Interest and How to Avoid Guys Who Can't Commit

By Bruce Bryans

Legal Disclaimer

My Free Gift to You

As a way of saying "thanks" for your purchase, I'm offering a free 10-lesson email course (and other assorted goodies) that are exclusive to my book readers. Each lesson reveals some of my best-kept dating secrets for cultivating **long-term attraction** with high-quality men.

You can access it at:

http://www.brucebryans.com/ecourse/

In this free course, you will not only learn the most high-value dating behaviours that make men burn with desire and desperate to commit to a woman, but you'll also learn how to confidently interact with men so that you can get the guy you want, keep him interested, and quickly weed out time-wasters, players, and men who'll never commit.

Again, you can access it at:

http://www.brucebryans.com/ecourse/

Table of Contents

Introduction 1

Chapter 1: When it's Really About Him and Not About You..11

Chapter 2: When His Struggles and Fears Hijack His Heart..35

Chapter 3: When Your Dating Habits Drive Him Away 49

Chapter 4: When He's Just Not Buying Whatever You're Selling 79

Chapter 5: When He Thinks He Can Do "Better" Than You..97

Chapter 6: How to Understand Men and the Way They Date 109

Chapter 7: How to Avoid the Pitfalls of Romantic Love 121

Chapter 8: How to Protect Your Dignity and Win with Men..131

Final Thoughts: A Tale of Two Love-Worthy Women 141

"When you make the man a "prize" that needs to be pursued, you run the risk of making him feel like less of a man. To him at least, it will feel as if you're trying to coerce him into a relationship. And when he feels as if he's being "sweetly" pressured into a commitment, your value as a long-term partner immediately drops in his eyes. This is one of the most common reasons why men pull away and suddenly disappear in the beginning stages of a blossoming romance."

~ **Bruce Bryans,** *How To Get A Man Without Getting Played*

Introduction

If you have ever dated a man before, it probably goes without saying that you've been in situations where men pulled away or suddenly lost interest in you without an explanation. You've probably been in situations where you felt hurt, disappointed, frustrated, and confused after a great guy lost interest in you even though he seemed so passionate in the beginning. On the other hand, you might have experienced the sadness, anger, distress, and utter shock that followed after your long-term boyfriend suddenly pulled away from you and unceremoniously ended the relationship. Don't worry; you're not alone. These kinds of experiences are common to ALL women who are (or were) actively engaged in the often-harrowing activity of finding Mr. Right.

Such incidents might have been few and far between for women dating fifty years ago. But in this day and age, having a man display a passionate interest at the beginning of a courtship only for him to eventually pull a Houdini and go "ghost" has become the norm for many women *(Ghost: when a man ends a courtship/ relationship by simply ignoring the woman and*

1

terminating all communications with her). And for various reasons, finding a sincere, deeply interested man who follows through on his passion throughout the course of a relationship seems to be as likely as winning the lottery; where you know it happens for some people, but you're thoroughly convinced that it might never be you.

Demystifying Male Romantic Interest

No matter your age, race, or social status, as a woman searching for Mr. Right you have probably had the misfortune of experiencing a myriad of situations where a man came on strong at first and eventually loss interest in you. For example, you might have met a handsome stranger or a friend-of-a-friend at a social gathering, one who practically begged you for your contact information and pulled out all the stops to get you to go out with him. Sensing his sincere interest in you, you took a chance on him and actually enjoyed the first, the second, and the third date with him. You had hoped that "this guy seems different from the rest" and that he "might actually be for real". You probably even thought to yourself that, "this might actually go somewhere!".

You date him for several weeks and things go extremely well. It almost feels like a romantic fantasy because of the passionate way he pursues you. Your initial reluctance quickly transforms into overzealous anticipation, as every moment with your Mr. McDreamy floods you with a breadth of emotions that makes you *feel* things you've never felt before (or haven't felt in a very long time). Sharing your emotional intensity, your new Prince Charming takes you on a special dinner date and begs you to be exclusive with him. In your excitement, you blurt out *"Yes!"* with so much enthusiasm that the people around you begin thinking he had just proposed to you.

However, after a few months of reciprocating his infatuated fervour where you gave him your all, squeezed the romance out of every available moment with him, and made him a major priority in your life, something begins to feel inexplicably wrong. You're not sure at first but you can sense it in your gut. You soon realize that Prince Charming doesn't call or text you as much as he used to. You also realize that he only spends time with you once or twice a week, where at first it had been almost every day. You become frustrated once you realize that at present, whenever Mr. McDreamy does make plans to go out with you, it's always at the last minute, and when you try to make plans with *him* he usually has some lame excuse as to why your plans won't work with his busy schedule.

You've been here before. And worse of all...you know what's possibly coming.

Naturally, being terrified of what transpired in your past (and short-lived) relationships, you do all that you possibly can to fill in the space your Prince Charming has created in the relationship. You surprise him at work with more romantic gestures. You send him even more cute little texts in order to gain his attention. You even do more favours for him, make yourself more available to him, and go above and beyond the call of duty in an attempt to meet his needs (whatever they are). And when that doesn't work, you become even more anxious, irritable, and sullen, which then compels you to badger your once-passionate pursuer weekly (if not daily) with passive-aggressive demands for his time and attention.

Naturally, when he fails to demonstrate his once-burning desire for you, in desperation you may find yourself overcome with the need to ask him questions pertaining to his lack of interest. Questions like:

- "What's wrong?"
- "Did I do something?"
- "How can we fix this?"
- "You're not the same anymore"
- "You're acting different", etc.

Yet in spite of all your trying, fighting, protesting, and romantic "bribery" he continues to pull even further away until he eventually punches you in the gut with a simple text message: "This isn't working."

Ouch.

As we all know, this is just one of the many scenarios a woman may find herself in if she does not understand the masculine mind, the way men fall in love, choose their mates, and navigate relationships. No woman can change the reality that any man, no matter how interested or invested he may first appear, can potentially pull away and suddenly lose interest in her at some point during their courtship. Although this is the reality, a woman can, in fact, change the way she deals with such situations in order to:

1. Prevent an eventual dismissal and pull her Prince Charming back to her, or...

2. Protect her dignity and command a man's respect if he attempts to disgracefully dismiss her (such as being dumped by text or worse...having a man

disappear).

Keep in mind that while you cannot control a man's behaviour, you can control your own. Only by controlling your own behaviour can you then *influence* a man to treat you in a way that is best befitting for a woman of your calibre. But in order to effectively influence a man's behaviour, a woman must possess a decent understanding of why men pull away and suddenly lose interest. When a woman possesses this knowledge about male behaviour, she will rarely find herself being caught off guard or feeling powerless when dealing with a disappearing man or one with waning romantic interest.

Sometimes a sincere beau who is pulling away will need to be reminded of your high-value. Thus, understanding why men lose interest and how to respond appropriately to his loss of interest can retrigger his attraction and compel him to pursue you for deeper emotional intimacy.

On the other hand, you might simply find yourself dating a man who wasn't right for you from the beginning. Thus, understanding the reasons why men lose interest and how to respond appropriately to such behaviour will help you to avoid chasing a man who was never right for you and who was probably never *that* interested in you.

Get Inside His Mind

The thing is, a woman can astronomically increase her chances of success with men and dating simply by doing one thing: Understanding men. When a woman truly understands male dating behaviour, she becomes

5

far more capable of handling a man when he starts to pull away, or worse, if he tries to unceremoniously dismiss her by ghosting her after several weeks of dating. When a woman truly understands male dating behaviour, she can respond to a man's waning romantic interest from a place of feminine poise and power rather than desperation, anxiety, and frantic fretting. Simply put, understanding men – how they think, how they date, and what they want (and want to avoid) when it comes to women and relationships – is the key to having immeasurable confidence in the midst of relationship uncertainty, especially in those cases when a man doesn't act in the way you expected him to.

The purpose of this book is to help you understand some of the most common reasons why men lose interest and to provide you with the keys to maintaining your poise and power whenever a man does withdraw emotionally or attempts to ghost you. By giving you unfiltered access to how men think, you will be able to easily recognize the natural push and pull of a man's romantic desire and respond to it effectively in order to keep the attention of the right man while avoiding dead-end relationships with men who just aren't that interested in you.

One Important Assumption

Before we go on, I wanted to note that as you read through this book please remind yourself that for the points herein we are going to assume that a man is *genuinely* interested in you and is not *consciously* trying to use or take advantage of you. This is very important to keep in mind as you read through this book because it will help you to better empathize with men as I reveal various things about their behavior.

I understand that for a woman, having a man pull away from you and disappear can be painful, especially if you took his bait, went against your misgivings, and invested your time, love, and emotions. But if you view each instance of this as an act of maliciousness and intent to harm you, you'll go into every new dating situation with a pessimistic view of men that could prove detrimental to your future dating success.

Therefore, for the sake of better understanding men, let's assume that the guys I'm discussing in this book aren't all players, pick-up artists, or narcissistic psychopaths unless it is specified in that particular section. Let's assume, from hereon in, that the guys I'm referring to are genuinely interested in you and also very prone to errors in judgment and decency (as are all human beings).

Sounds fair? Good. Let's move on.

The Women that Need this Book

If you find that you have little to no problem attracting men, but seem to have a ton of issues getting them to commit or even keeping them interested in you longer than a few weeks, this book is for you. If you also seem to have trouble deciphering why the guys you date continue to pull away, withdraw emotionally, or worse...disappear without a trace even though you *thought* things were going well in the "relationship", this book is for you. Lastly, if men do pursue you passionately at first and beg you to be their girlfriend, only to lead you into dead-end, on-and-off relationships where you're never sure if they really want to be with you or not…this book is for you.

Now, even though we have defined the problem, we still need to properly define the kind of woman I truly want to help with this book. I write <u>all of my books</u> with a particular woman in mind; those with sincere hearts, lots of love and respect to give, and who have a deep desire to find a high-quality, commitment-ready man to build a life with. I do this to ensure that the advice I give pertaining to how men think is not abused or misused by women.

With all that said, here are two ways to know if this book will benefit you:

1. You want to attract and keep the attention of a high-quality man (a man with high self-esteem, ambition, leadership qualities, compassion, cherishes commitment, has high-standards for himself, defends his personal boundaries, knows what he wants, speaks his mind, understands the value of relationships, and exudes masculine, sexual confidence).

2. You want to pursue and nurture a *loving relationship that can lead to marriage* with such a man.

If you're not interested in dating guys that will hold you to a high but reasonable standard (meaning he won't tolerate flaky or disrespectful behavior) or if you're not interested in securing a serious relationship with a masculine man who wants and values commitment…this book is not for you. If you want to attract one-night stands, so called "players", or forty something year-old bad boys who think commitment is just another curse word…this book is not for you.

Understanding the major reasons why men pull away will help you to hold on to your power whenever a man does begin to withdraw from you in a relationship. And if used properly, this power will prove useful in attracting a man back to you if he's starting to pull away, and it will also keep you immeasurably confident and perfectly poised whenever a guy attempts to ghost you.

With the information in this book you'll actually be able to read a man *like* a book. So be sure your heart is in the right place when it comes to dating and relating with men, because while this knowledge might be beneficial to a woman with nobler aims, it could also be dangerous in hands of a woman with cruel intentions. Now, if you fit the former description and are ready to have more confidence and power with men and dating, I encourage you to read on.

Chapter 1:

When it's Really About Him and Not About You

1

The timing was bad...for him.

One of the top (and perhaps the most common) reasons why men pull away from a blossoming relationship is because of "bad timing". When a man is at a place in his life where he has neither the need nor desire for a girlfriend, there's very little a woman can do to convince or *coerce* him to change his mind. In situations like this, it's better for a woman to focus her energy on making room in her life for more insistent (and commitment-minded) suitors as opposed to wasting that energy trying helplessly to convince the man in question that she's worth reconsidering.

The worst-case scenario for a woman in this situation is when she, because of her lack of understanding when it comes to men, becomes *addicted* to trying to please a man in order to keep his attention and draw him back to her. Unfortunately, as any woman who has ever been in this situation can admit, this sort of over-devotion to a man who's "not ready" for a commitment never works.

Getting His Life Together

As sad as it may sound, if you've had men bail on you after spending inordinate amounts of time with you and getting to know you intimately, I'd wager that at least six times out of ten it might have been due to bad timing (for him at least). What's worse is that if you're in your twenties to early-thirties (or dating men in their twenties), you're likely to come across more men like this than you'd care to meet.

I remember a time when I was at a small gathering where a group of guys (at the time we were all in our late twenties to early thirties) had gotten together to celebrate a friend's marriage proposal to his long-term girlfriend. Naturally, because drinks were flowing and we were feeling pretty festive, we all began to "open up" (by guy standards at least) about women, dating, marriage, and everything in between. During this outing, one of the guys, let's call him Darren, started to talk about his regrets for not locking things down with an old girlfriend of his.

Now at this point in his life, Darren was very successful in his career and spent the majority of his time doing important international work that required travel and mingling with dignitaries and diplomats. He expressed that while he was pleased with where he was career-wise, he did wish things had turned out differently with this particular ex-girlfriend.

He mentioned that a few years prior, they had ended their long-term relationship simply due to the fact that he wasn't ready to take things to the next level (i.e. – marriage). While they were dating, he wasn't where he wanted to be both in his career and finances and therefore had difficulty pouring his all into the relationship. The intriguing thing was that as he spoke, there was an obvious sadness in his voice. As he explained his regret you could see his eyes wander off as if he was trying to figure out for himself if there was a way that things could have turned out differently between them.

As a man, I can clearly admit that Darren's case is not unique. Most well-meaning men have good intentions and would love to feel "secure" enough with where they are in their lives to take a woman seriously. We'd love to be able to see into the future and believe that in-spite of our apparent lack of success, status, or prestige we could be confident enough (or just "enough" in general) to commit our all to the woman we truly do love and want. In an ideal world, we'd love to be able to easily ignore the anxieties that make us pull away from a good thing – but life is rarely that simple.

Which leads me to a very important point…

Don't Devaluate a Man's Doubts

There is one ENORMOUS benefit to you when a man who's "not ready" begins pulling away from you, and it's this: If he is really "not ready" **and his doubts are overwhelming**, you've saved yourself from an even worse and more unexpected break-up in the future. Why? It's because when a man honestly feels that the timing is off for him, it takes an enormous amount of willpower and emotional resilience to overcome the "what ifs" at the back of his mind, no matter how devoted he is to you.

I'm convinced that most women have no idea how difficult it is for a man to overcome his doubts about the future, even if he truly does love and adore the woman he's dating. I'm also convinced that most women have no idea the amount of pressure men naturally place on themselves if things fall apart with a woman they care about. The thing is, if a man chooses to ignore his anxieties and commits to you in-spite of his fear, there's always a chance that he might remain in constant doubt of what he could have become, attained, or experienced *without you*. If a man truly isn't ready to commit to you but still decides to do so, there's always a chance that he may doubt who he is while he's with you. And the reason this doubt exists is because he committed to you before ever knowing (or realizing) what he could have become or achieved on his own.

I say all this to help bring about a paradigm-shift in your thinking in regards to male behavior. When a guy you're dating consistently pulls away to the point where you would have to learn Geisha level seduction skills just to keep him interested, you might be better off just letting him be. Although it still hurts and might make you question your worth, in most cases (if not all of them), when a man pulls away and disappears because of "bad timing", it's for your own good.

When "Bad Timing" Means Something Else

Now, another important point to consider is that for a man, "bad timing" could mean many different things. And while some of those things might appear selfish to a woman (especially if he's been leading you on), some things are actually legitimate reasons that could keep a man up at night. So, for your future reference (and perhaps present amusement), here's a list of things that a man could be experiencing to make him *feel* as if the timing if off for him:

- He's nowhere near where he wants to be with his career, finances, or social status, and feels unworthy to take on a serious commitment.

- He's not emotionally mature enough to handle a serious relationship with a self-possessed

15

woman. (These are usually the self-absorbed "me-me-me" types of men that have "better" relationships with women with weak or non-existent boundaries.)

- He's at a point in his life where he has unmitigated access to women who are both interested in him and willing to keep things casual. (He might have led you on hoping to add you to his "harem" of ready, willing, and clueless women.)

- He's not that interested in you and therefore doesn't feel any sense of urgency or need to pursue you.

- He's still madly in love with an ex-girlfriend or is still emotionally sore due to previously ending a long-term relationship with a woman he deeply cared about.

- He feels threatened by your level of financial success, social status, or simply due to the fact that you "have your life together" and he doesn't.

- He sincerely doesn't know what he wants but he respects you enough to not waste anymore of your time.

As you can see from the list above, "bad timing", though a common reason for a man's waning interest, is still a blanket term to describe many different issues. Sure, a man may simply tell you (if he tells you at all) that he's "just not ready" as a way to avoid the truth of what's really going on. But for the most part, if he's communicated that he's not ready, whether verbally or through his on-going disappearing acts, consider yourself fortunate – especially if he acts this way earlier than later while dating him.

If He Wasn't Ready Why Would He Lead Me On?

Now having a man pull away and suddenly lose interest all because of "bad timing" can leave a woman even more hurt and confused. Especially, when considering how much time and energy she might have invested in the man in question. For a woman, "bad timing" is one of the most bewildering reasons why men pull away because it leaves her wondering one simple question: *"If he wasn't ready for a relationship…why would he lead me on in the first place?"*

The thing is, even though men are more than able to commit to a woman once certain conditions in their life are met (most of which will have nothing to do with you, by the way), they will not directly *tell you* that no matter what you do or say, you're not going to get the commitment you want. Few guys will rarely ever come out and *inform you* when you're not the right girl for them or that now isn't the right time for them to take a woman seriously.

A man might be fully aware that he's not ready for anything serious and lead you on anyway because for him at least, there is little if any downside to dating for dating sake. Because a man can achieve higher levels of status and socioeconomic success *with time*, "time" itself is **rarely** a factor in dating for men. Add to this the fact that a man becomes more experienced and therefore more successful with the opposite sex the more he dates around, which over time improves his ability to attract more seemingly "unattainable" women in the future. So from a man's standpoint, "time" is more of a boon to him in the mating market rather than a disadvantage.

On the other hand, for women seeking serious commitment, any time spent stuck in dead-end relationships with ambivalent men represents time not spent with the man of their dreams. It represents time not spent dating for marriage, and for many women, starting a family. It may even represent the loss of self-esteem, reputation, and personal dignity, especially if a woman habitually dates dissolute, irresolute, predatory, or abusive (whether physically or emotionally) men.

The reality is, men rarely ever *inform* women when they're not ready for commitment, both prior to a budding romance and even AFTER it's fallen apart. If he chooses not to inform her that he pulled away or disappeared due to "bad timing", this lack of an explanation usually creates a deep feeling of ambiguity in a woman. Unfortunately, because of this sleep-depriving ambiguity, if a woman is prone to self-delusion she'll be more likely to *rationalize* a man's "I'm not ready" behavior as him telling her: "I need you to convince me."

The ambiguity of the situation creates a fog of confusion in her mind that compels her to try harder to make Mr. I'm-Not-Ready believe she's his exception. I'm sure I don't have to tell you that the only relationship a woman will end up with from chasing a man in this fashion is one where she becomes nothing more than a friend-with-benefits. Don't become a friend-with-benefits. That is of course, if you're more interested in dating men who want to *claim* you as their girlfriend.

2

He's a "passion junkie" – a man who loves the chase but abhors commitment.

The ugly reality for women (since they're usually on the receiving end of such behaviour) is that there are men out there who enjoy the process of seducing women, but have zero interest in actually cultivating relationships with them. Of course, I'm sure most women have already arrived at this conclusion, but I believe I should mention it anyway and more importantly, explain why this is.

Although you may come across guys who do this sort of thing unconsciously (meaning they unknowingly lose interest in a woman the minute she's been "caught"), more often than not, the guys who exhibit this sort of behaviour are fully aware of what they're doing. In our modern vernacular, we call such men "players", or, if they're particularly specialized and purposeful in seducing women for the sake of it, we might consider them pick-up-artists.

As I mentioned in the beginning of this book, I wanted to focus solely on explaining why a man who is **genuinely interested in you** might pull away and disappear. A player or pick-up-artist is not genuinely interested in YOU, only what pleasures he can extract *from* you. Therefore, if you happen to find yourself dating a player or pick-up-artist and he disappears, don't be surprised because he is merely following his unique dating protocol. You can be hurt, angry, or even disgusted that you fell for him, but don't insult your intelligence by being surprised (especially after reading this book).

He Wants Your Desire...Not Your Love

Now, when a passion junkie (not a player or pick-up-artist) who at least *thinks* he's genuinely interested in you pulls away and disappears, it's either because of one of two reasons:

1. He's addicted to romantic novelty and loses interest the minute it inevitably wears off, or...

2. His self-esteem is intrinsically linked to how thoroughly he's seduced a woman; meaning he won't stop pursuing you *until* he's been satisfied (physically and psychologically) that you've developed an unwavering desire for him.

In both instances the passion junkie is the guy who goes hard in the beginning of a romance in order to overwhelm you with amorous feelings, which makes it difficult for you to see him for what he really is. And while it's true that men do love the chase aspect of wooing a woman, passion junkies are the extremists among us. They always want what they can't have and never seem to be satisfied with whatever they end up with, at least when it comes to women and dating.

The biggest problem with dating a guy like this is that as soon as your attention becomes fully focused on him, he loses interest. So long as you're paying more attention to what a man does as opposed to what he says, you can easily discover whether or not you're dealing with a passion junkie. A guy like this is easy to spot as a relationship develops because his interest in you will be very unstable and heavily dependent on the level of attention he's getting from you. The more attention he gets from you, the less he'll want to be with you. The less attention you give him, the more insistent he will be to win your desire (notice I didn't say win your "heart", because that's not what he's after).

Keeping the Passion Junkie Hooked

Sometimes guys like this can be "seduced" into a relationship if you're willing to put up with the amount of legwork necessary to keep them consistently engaged. Dating strategies like *playing* hard-to-get throughout the entire course of a courtship may work on such men because it feeds their need to keep the hunt going strong. Personally, I think you'll either burn yourself out or drive yourself insane trying to keep a man like this interested for the long-term. Of course, if you fancy the thought of having to methodically "game" a man into a commitment from the first date up until marriage, the passion junkie might be the right guy for you.

So consider yourself fortunate if you realize sooner than later that your Mr. McDreamy is only interested in the chase. The faster you figure this out the less time you'll end up wasting on men like this. While it might be irritating at first when you realize that a man is losing interest in you simply because you've begun to reciprocate his attention, it's still a lot less maddening than prolonging a love affair that has an extremely high chance of ending in a dead-end relationship.

If a man fails to show a clear and consistent interest in you, the kind of interest that doesn't waver the minute you begin to reciprocate in kind, you might be dealing with a novelty-seeking passion junkie. Yes, while it's true that you may sometimes have to pull away from a man in order to give him the space he needs to miss you and pursue you once again, such artful tactics of seduction should only have to be used sparingly. If it appears that you'll have to use this tactic every other week just to keep a man interested in you, you can be sure that you're dealing with a passion junkie, and therefore…a waste of time.

3

He had placed you on a pedestal, only to eventually find out that you were…human.

Due to an unfortunate combination of pop cultural influences, feelings of self-entitlement, and good old-fashioned ignorance, some men have the bad habit of placing the women they're really attracted to on pedestals. Guys who unknowingly place women on pedestals (the ones they're attracted to at least) always end up disappointed when the woman they're dating fails to match up to the ideal they're holding on to.

You may be familiar with this situation if you have ever had a man pursue you passionately in the beginning dating stages only to fervently pull away and disappear later on once he got to know the *real*, unfiltered you. Experiences like this often leave a woman feeling confused as she helplessly wonders if it was something she said or did to turn off her Mr. McDreamy.

This type of dating situation might also leave a woman feeling embittered once she realizes that she fell for another insistent romancer and allowed herself to succumb to the idea that *"this guy could actually be for real this time."* Sadly, guys who habitually do this are never "for real" simply due to the fact that they tend to place the women they date on tiny, unstable "pedestals of perfection." And as is their nature, once it becomes apparent that the lady they've placed on this pedestal is prone to error, gross behavior, misjudgment, and vice just like any other human being, they lose interest in her.

He's Temporarily Blinded by a Fog of Love

When a man like this first meets you, he's awestruck by your physical beauty and the female mystery that is YOU. He doesn't know what to expect from you, and the novelty of a *new* woman floods his brain with "love chemicals" like oxytocin and dopamine. The possibility of a passionate love affair with this new woman also ups his expectations and clouds his judgment even further. Heavily blinded by a hormone induced "love fog", in his eyes you can do no wrong (for the moment at least). And it's at this point where a man becomes more than willing to put up with the natural complications that might arise from romantically pursuing that irresistible quarry known as woman.

Then...it happens.

Somewhere along the way, the "love fog" lifts from his eyes and he now has a front row seat to the spectacular performance that is YOU. The "YOU" includes those character flaws, annoying habits, and quirky idiosyncrasies only a mother (or the right man) could love. Things like your irrational passion for rehabilitating stray and abused dogs (you have five and they all sleep in or around your bed), your secret collection of ugly but oh-so-comfortable granny underwear, your crazy habit of yelling at people who chew too loudly, or the unforgivable sin that you just don't "get" *Star Wars* will now be out in the open at this point in the relationship.

Though he was once oblivious to such things because of the "love fog" or ignorant of them because you tried to put your best foot forward, he now has unfiltered access to who you are at your core – the good, the bad, and the granny underwear ugly.

No matter how well we try to put our best foot forward when trying to cultivate a romantic connection with someone new, our insecurities, anxieties, neurosis, and character flaws will eventually surface. Of course, there's nothing wrong with this since it's only a part of the human experience. But the problem arises when your new Mr. McDreamy SUDDENLY realizes that you're not as perfectly and as wonderfully made as he had previously envisioned.

It's at this point that he will begin to pull away from you, feeling both disheartened and confused with himself because he really thought you were flawless and had it all. Once he's seen enough of the real you, your once passionate and insistent pursuer will disappear into the shadows where he'll ignore your phone calls, disregard your texts, and shake his head contemptuously while snubbing your Facebook messages.

Guys like this pull away because to them, you've lost the allure, mystery, novelty, and most importantly, perfection, that drove them to passionately pursue you in the beginning stages of the romance. And once they've thoroughly convinced themselves that you're "not that special" anymore, they disappear and cease all contact out of sheer confusion and/or disappointment. They're confused because they really thought that what they felt at the beginning was real to them, and disappointment (mostly in themselves) for feeling as if they did, in fact, lead you on.

Men with Immature Dating Habits

Assuming this is the reason why a man pulled a Houdini on you, if you have sat up at night wondering how could he do so without so much as an explanation, I'll tell you: Men, in general, aren't very introspective with their emotions and even fewer men even care to understand their emotions. Unless a man has had extensive dating experience or has been informed on these sorts of things, he probably has NO IDEA why he acts this way.

This is the ugly truth.

Now I can assure you that ALL men feel this loss of allure and mystery at some point, but only the guys who are **emotionally mature** and understand that no relationship retains its novelty forever (at least not without effort from both individuals) will stick around to create something deeper and more meaningful with you.

If you'd like to keep your experiences with such men to a minimal, you should be more cautious when dating certain types of younger men (think early to mid-twenties) or much older, stubborn men with well-entrenched lifestyles who are more likely to have impossible standards for the women they date. Granted, I'm not saying that a younger man or a much older gentleman in his fifties is incapable of seeing a woman as a perfectly beautiful yet flawed human creature. I'm just saying that from my experience and observation, younger, inexperienced guys searching for "The One" can be a bit naïve and overly optimistic when it comes to dealing with women. Older gentlemen who have been in few if any stable romantic relationships at all tend to be a little less flexible and forgiving with women. Again, these aren't hard-and-fast rules, just general observations a woman should consider when navigating the dating marketplace.

Does He Want a Real Woman or a Disney Princess?

The key to finding out if a man is interested in dating a real human woman is to become a master at extracting deep-rooted character-revealing information from men as early as possible during your interactions with them. Ideally, you should do this WAY before you *allow* yourself to become smitten by a man's insistent charms and romantic fervor.

As early as possible, when you're getting to know a guy, ask him exactly what is it he's looking for in a potential girlfriend. If you're afraid of scaring him away with such questions earlier on (don't be), you might want to try a cleverer approach for extracting information from this man.

For instance, as you converse with him, incorporate a hint of feminine coquettishness and illustrate a genuine interest in what he has to say. Men love to be seen as interesting in the same way women love being desirable. When he relaxes and begins to open up a bit more, ensure that you engage him emotionally (using your feminine body language, mesmerizing eye contact, girlish laughter, etc.) while casually asking for his opinions about women and relationships.

Listen to him intently, and allow him to wax poetic about what he loves and wants in a woman, particularly a girlfriend. The things he reveals might quickly inform you whether you're dating a man with a mature view of women and relationships or one who is still waiting on his Disney princess.

Is he overly optimistic and believes that there's only one "soul mate" out there for each of us? Or is he hopeful but realistic in his romantic desires? Is he looking for a woman to complement his busy, well-entrenched life? Or is he looking for someone to share his life with and create new memories? Really pay attention to him and listen for those subtle distinctions that reveal if he might place you on a pedestal or if he already has.

I should note that you should take extra caution if you notice that he consistently attempts to change the subject, distract you with charming banter, or chooses to ignore your question. Humorous misdirection, flirtatious dismissiveness, and masculine aloofness are a man's best tools to keep a woman helplessly interested in him while also keeping her completely in the dark of his true intentions. Be insistent at getting to know the REAL him

before you allow yourself to swoon for him. Because if he's the kind of man who bails once he finally meets the REAL you, you will only end up wasting your time.

4

He needs time away from you and the relationship to reconnect with his masculine identity.

In his bestselling book, *Men Are from Mars, Women Are from Venus*, author John Gray dedicates an entire section to the withdrawal behavior of men. In this section, he refers to this behavior as the "Rubber Band" [1] concept, and explains it simply as being a part of a man's natural intimacy cycle where he needs to pull away from a relationship in order to reconnect with his masculine identity.

According to Gray, this is a normal phase that men go through, especially when they've developed an intimate relationship with a woman. And it's in this phase where men tend to disconnect from the woman they love in order to focus on those things that make him feel more like a man. Which are essentially those very things that make him a good provider and partner. Once a man *has* had the chance to reconnect with his masculine identity he will feel ready to experience more and perhaps even deeper intimacy with his woman.

Gray suggests that men sometimes pull away from relationships after experiencing the closeness and intimacy of a partnership, the "we state", in order to get more of the "me state", where a man needs to reconnect with his more masculine, independent, and autonomous side. He likens a man experiencing intimacy with a woman to an all-you-can-eat buffet, where once he's become "full" he'll need some time and space away from her in order to develop a renewed hunger for her intimacy.

Dealing with the "Rubber Band" Man

Naturally, when a seemingly happy and once content man begins to pull away, a woman's immediate response is to become frantic, fretful, and filled with panic. She starts off by trying to find the reason for his loss of interest, blaming everything from herself and the mistakes she *thinks* she's made with him to his *supposed* lack of clarity, thought, and consistency in displaying his love and devotion for her. Acting this way with a man who simply needs more of his "me state" is a surefire way to turn his short-term need to pull away into a long-term desire to keep away from you indefinitely. What you want to do in this particular scenario is simply this: Try a little tenderness.

Instead of rewarding his withdrawal with *more* favors, acts of love, physical intimacy, gifts, etc., simply maintain your poise and position and give him the space he needs. Don't become a doormat and attempt to pull him back by overinvesting in the relationship. This will only create more frustration on both sides; he will feel stifled by your attempts to "buy" his love, and you will become even more distraught by his indifference.

Resist the urge to emotionally guilt-trip him into showing you just how much he cares. And more importantly, resist the temptation to fill in the silent and empty places his withdrawal has created in the relationship. Don't chase him with your love, as doing so won't earn you his pity, it will only earn you his repulsion. Trying to pull him back to you by pursuing him will eventually cause his "rubber band" to break since he will feel as if you don't trust his devotion and that he cannot make you happy.

Nurturing His Confidence in the Commitment

If he's not aware that his feelings are a natural part of his intimacy cycle, when a man pulls away in this type of scenario he may struggle with feelings of self-doubt towards his actual feelings for you. What this means is that although he <u>does</u> love you and sincerely wants to be with you, this "phase" he's going through might make him more susceptible to *how YOU feel about his commitment*. Your response to his withdrawal must inspire his confidence as opposed to his deepest, unmentioned fears if you want him to quickly come back to you.

For example, if you become so anxious and frantic that you cast blame on him, because he's in a more susceptible state you'll nourish the self-doubts he has about his commitment to you. If he already struggles with the thought that he won't be able to make you happy, casting blaming on him will only confirm his self-doubts and solidify his negative beliefs concerning the relationship. Or, if you become so fearful and desperate that you demand more of his time and greater displays of his love and devotion, again, you'll only end up solidifying his self-doubts as he'll be led to believe things like:

- "She doesn't believe in the love I have for her. Nothing I do will ever make her happy."

- "I'm not enough for her. She will always want MORE than I can give."

- "She doesn't respect my boundaries and my masculine need to feel free."

- "She only wants what's best for her. She only wants me because of _____."

- "She'll be miserable without me. I don't want her to feel miserable, but right now I feel so…trapped."

Yes, men who love you will sometimes struggle with such thoughts. And the often-vulnerable state of the "rubber band" phase creates the perfect opportunity for you to either nurture his self-confidence or solidify his self-doubts about being with you. Remember, never let a man realize that his pulling away immediately pulls you apart, as it will only result in him feeling trapped and suffocated by your love.

Keeping Contact with a "Rubber Band" Man

In most cases, if a man is pulling away from you it's best not to make any efforts to get in touch or contact him. However, because men who withdraw to reconnect with their masculine identity are usually in good relationships with solid foundations, it's still okay to keep in contact with them so long as your contacting is

31

not overbearing and lacking purpose.

For example, if your boyfriend of two years is clearly withdrawing from you and has been creating some distance, don't chase or nag him with incessant phone calls or texts. Contact him with the aim to keep the lines of communication open, and ensure that you have an actual *reason* for contacting him.

Let's say he often helped you with a certain errand, like getting your car maintenance done. If that's the case, it may be okay to remind him that your car is due for an appointment and give him the option of assisting you with it like he's always done in the past. Remember, you're not trying to "win" him back, because that assumes that you've "lost" him or are in the process of "losing" him. Simply contact him purposefully with a no-pressure request or question to keep the lines of communication open and then give him space to miss you and come back.

By the way, while you're doing all this, ensure that you're not waiting patiently beside the phone for him to call or text you. This WILL drive you insane and make your communication attempts appear excruciatingly desperate. Instead of waiting on him, get reacquainted with yourself and the things/people in your life you've neglected due to being consumed in your romantic relationship. Get busy with life and lavish your love on pastimes, people, and constructive pursuits instead of letting it waste away during those inevitable lulls you might experience whenever a man withdraws.

Is He "Rubber Banding" or Disbanding the Relationship?

Now, it's important to note that while it is normal for a man to withdraw emotionally from a relationship to reconnect with his masculine identity, this sort of thing does not happen in the **earlier stages** of a relationship. A man who withdraws from you after two weeks of dating is not "rubber banding", he's just not that interested. A man who withdraws from you after two months of very casual dating is not "rubber banding", he's just not that interested.

Another important thing to consider is that a man who pulls away because he needs to reconnect with his masculinity is doing so because **he actually needs to reconnect with his masculinity**, nothing more, nothing less. In other words, there's nothing inherently wrong with you or the relationship, he just needs to get his needs met by creating some emotional and perhaps even physical space away from you. Don't be tempted to ease your gut-felt concerns about a man by immediately telling yourself that he's simply "rubber banding" when in fact, he might actually be pulling away for some other reason (like the ones listed throughout this book).

The reason I'm mentioning this is because many women, in an attempt to overlook the serious issues they're facing with men and dating, have come across the "rubber band" concept and used it as a panacea to explain and deal with a man's ambivalent and/or emotionally abusive behavior towards them. Don't do this. You have to be very objective and clear-sighted in how you judge and appraise male behavior if you want to properly diagnose your situation with a man.

So while the man you've been happily with for nine months or two years might be pulling away from you as a means to reconnect with his masculine self, if you're in a relationship that's barely off the ground, has serious on-going conflicts, or one that has always had a rocky foundation, resist the temptation to label your guy's behavior as "rubber banding". Because in situations like these, chances are that there's some other issue at hand rather than him just wanting to have more man-cave time.

Reference: [1] Gray, John. "Chapter 6/Men Are Like Rubber Bands." *Men Are from Mars, Women Are from Venus: The Classic Guide to Understanding the Opposite Sex*, HarperCollins.

Chapter 2:

When His Struggles and Fears Hijack His Heart

5

He's had a major and overwhelmingly stressful change suddenly occur in his life.

Some women have difficulty accepting the fact that a major change or stressful problem in a man's life can very suddenly derail a romantic relationship. Things like a sudden career change, personal debt, family illness/crisis, friendship betrayals, business failures, strong feelings of purposelessness, crisis of religious faith, and embarrassing health/psychological challenges all have the potential to make a man turn his focus on himself and his problems. This inward focus may cause a man to neglect a very promising romantic relationship. If the guy you're dating begins to pull away and eventually implode a relationship after experiencing a sudden and stressful change in his life, in cases like this it may be safe to believe him if he says: *"It's not you…it's me."*

Interestingly, I've noticed that women tend to vastly underestimate how crippling certain problems can be to a man's self-confidence. These are the kinds of problems that make a man *unsure* of himself and where he is in life. I've also noticed that a woman might underestimate the amount of time a man may require to "fix" the problem (assuming it is fixable) in order to place his attention back on a blossoming relationship. Unfortunately, these underestimations tend to cause women to have unrealistic expectations when it comes to men and relationships.

Don't Become a Man's Saviour

Here's the thing you MUST know about men: We aren't as quick as women usually are to "share the burdens" we experience in life with our friends and family. Generally, we tend to want to figure it out on our own first and exhaust our options before turning towards outside resources for assistance. Where women sometimes go wrong is that they try to become a source of assistance for men who might be going through a stressful situation. While there's nothing wrong with making yourself available as a source of help, some women have the bad habit of making themselves a man's saviour because of their love for or premature devotion to a man.

By making yourself a man's saviour you might actually *train him* to become overly dependent on you. Even though the idea of a man "needing" you might sound appealing at first, becoming a man's saviour will lead you into one of two situations: 1. You might find yourself in a situation in which you're always 'the rock' in the relationship, as opposed to *him* being 'the rock', or 2. You may end up as nothing more than a man's 'stepping stone' woman or worse...a 'starter wife.'

If you make a man so dependent on you that you become 'the rock' in the relationship, any attempt to change this dynamic might be met with fierce defiance, especially if he's gotten accustomed to having you as his private little problem solver. And ending up as a man's 'stepping stone' woman is just as bad (if not worse), since a man's commitment to you WILL have an expiry date.

In my book, _Never Chase Men Again_, I point out that women should avoid becoming a man's 'stepping stone' if they truly want to avoid wasting their time in one of the most miserable dead-end relationships imaginable. I discuss that being a man's 'stepping stone' means to him that you're nothing more than a _means_ to an _end_. The 'stepping stone' woman is the kind of woman who blindly sticks by and supports her man to _her_ bitter end. And her bitter end eventually arrives when the guy she's been supporting leaves her for his 'mountain' woman (the woman a man eventually pursues and marries when he feels as if he's finally "arrived" in life and wants a "trophy" to prove it). Obviously, becoming a man's rock, stepping stone, or any other geological formation for that matter is not a good idea. So think twice before you over-extend your womanly support and kindness to help solve a man's problems.

Knowing When to Stay and When to Go

Now I'm not going to sugar coat it, but the main problem for a woman in this situation (where his stress is affecting the relationship) is not whether or not a man might truly be interested in her enough to work things out together. The main problem is how honest she's going to be with herself. What I mean is, you might meet a great guy who has all the qualities you want in a man, but if he's going through an especially difficult period in his life, one that makes being in a serious relationship more of a hassle than anything else, then you might be better off taking your business elsewhere. If patience isn't one of your strongest virtues or if your biological clock is ringing loudly, dating a man who's unable to focus on a romantic relationship will be an exercise in insanity for the both of you.

Still, suggesting that you "take your business elsewhere" is easy to say when you're just getting to know a guy and things are still in their infancy. But if you've been dating a man consistently and even exclusively for several months, leaving the relationship for greener pastures won't be that easy (or even that honourable in some cases).

So what's a girl to do? Simple really. If you've decided that he's worth the effort and his particular problems aren't beyond your capacity to work through with him (in the event he actually *wants* your assistance), simply be there for him and offer him support so long as he's **aggressively proactive** about helping himself.

This is a better strategy then pressuring him to open up if you have noticed that he has become distant, distracted, and seemed to be pulling away. It's also a better strategy then trying to help him when he either hasn't asked for your help or he doesn't yet trust you on that level to be receptive to your support. Pushing him to "open up" to you, begging him to "let you in", or chasing him with support that either encroaches on his personal boundaries or emasculates him will only push him further and further away until he realizes that you are just another source of unnecessary stress in his life.

Be patient with him and create opportunities for him to open up. When he finally does open up, ensure that you listen to him empathically (a rare and essential communication skill for earning a man's trust and being able to positively influence him). Doing so will open him up even more because he will *feel* as if you truly understand what he's going through and that his well-being is important to you. When a man *feels* that you just "get him" on this level, he's far more likely to open up to your assistance and/or advice.

I admit, this is a difficult issue to navigate, but so long as you're fully aware of how men think and how they handle their emotions, you will make better decisions and therefore increase your chances of success.

The magic in giving a man the space and respect he needs to reveal himself to you is that over time you'll become a source of strength and support like none other in his life. It's this sort of feminine tenderness and emotional intimacy that will win his heart over time, as he won't be able to comprehend why he trusts you the way he does. And believe me, when a man reaches a point where he cannot fathom the reason why he deeply trusts a woman the way he does, she becomes an irreplaceable part of his life.

6

The fear of him losing his freedom suddenly kicked in and went into overdrive.

A man may truly love you, want to be with you, and

even express his desire to marry you in the near future only to suddenly go South Pole COLD on you without so much as a warning. Where he had once been so romantically insistent with you, his passion has now seemed to fade into nothingness. And where he was so excited and progressive about building a life together, he now gets irritated, angry, or even distant whenever you attempt to spend more time with him or bring up anything that has to do with marriage.

If you've ever had a passionate, marriage-minded man go cold on you even though the relationship seemed to be progressing nicely, chances are that somewhere along the way the fear of him losing his freedom began to overpower all sense of reason. This is one of the more unfortunate situations a woman might find herself in because it usually happens after several long months or in some cases, even years of dating.

How Men Derail Their Own Passion

When a once passionate and marriage-minded man suddenly switches from hot to cold, many women in these situations usually have NO IDEA what's going on in a man's mind. What's even worse is that they usually have no clue how to deal effectively with the situation. Instead of giving their suddenly cold Mr. McDreamy the time and space he needs to miss them, many women in these situations tend to become frantic, fearful, and full of anxiety which then compels them to pursue their guy in hopes of keeping him from falling away. Of course, I don't have to tell you that this only makes things worse.

But what's really happening in cases like this? Well, it's simple really. A man might believe you are "The One" and even date you like he'd never let you go with the thought that, *"Hey, I could actually see myself marrying this girl."* However, when the relationship begins to progress so that the possibility of marriage is becoming more and more real, there will be a moment where a simple but powerful passion-derailing thought suddenly hits him like a runaway freight train. And that thought is simply this: *"What the heck am I doing?"*

This thought, this very simple thought, leads a man down a treacherous, terror-stricken rabbit hole of negative emotions that bring up his worse fears, doubts, and insecurities about getting married (at least, getting married at this particular time in his life). It doesn't matter how compatible you two are or how good the romance is. If he allows the seeds of this thought to take root and bear fruit in his mind, your future with him is as good as dead.

This thought usually first arises during some event or occasion where he realizes that there are still things about his unmarried/past-single life status that he cannot see himself living without. He might be spending a night with his friends at a party remembering the "good old days" and the thought suddenly hits him that he will never ever be able to fully enjoy nights like the "good old days" ever again. He might be walking with you through the shopping mall to check out engagement rings when a cold terror suddenly grips him and causes him to act inexplicably disinterested and callous. You might have even travelled together to some exotic foreign locale only for him to realize in quiet desperation, that the world is awash with beautiful women he never knew existed.

I could go on, but I think you get the point.

The full myriad of reasons why a man might be terrified, anxious, or hesitant about getting married are beyond the scope of this book, but in this particular situation, where a married-minded man suddenly goes cold, the underlying reason for his sudden behaviour is, as I mentioned before, the result of the fear of him losing his freedom.

Of course, you might attempt to comfort yourself with the notion that you'd rather not be with a guy who experiences these kinds of terrors anyway. You may think that a man who truly loves you enough to want to marry you would never experience these sought of fears or think such things.

Don't be fooled, my dear.

Out of love and respect for their wives and girlfriends' feelings and self-esteem, men will RARELY, if ever, reveal the kinds of insecurities and doubts that I'm mentioning within this book. So don't think for a moment that your boyfriend of eleven months or your soon-to-be fiancé of two years haven't experienced at some point or another, the inner struggles I'm revealing to you.

Overcoming the Doubt

The truth is that many men (if not all) do feel these strong negative emotions and they do think such things. But the fact remains that some guys who experience "the fear" get married anyway and even go on to enjoy happy marriages. But what makes this particular group of men want to?

Well, the main reason they do so is because they're mature enough to work through their fears and anxieties in order to reach the truth within, which is that they truly do love this woman and want to be with her above others, **in-spite of their fears and insecurities**.

When the *"What the heck am I doing?"* question does pop into a man's mind, he finds himself at a crossroads where one path leads towards marriage and the other leads toward freedom. Whether he chooses to stay with you or implode the relationship is heavily dependent on the amount of love AND respect he has for you, the quality of your relationship, and most importantly, **where he is in his life at the moment** (refer to point <u>number one</u>). It takes a lot of maturity for him to move a relationship forward in-spite of his groundless fears. This is why it's always in a woman's best interest to test a man's emotional maturity as early as possible in a relationship.

If you've never had a marriage-minded man go cold on you and bail, consider yourself most fortunate. For one thing, it's certainly not pretty when "the fear" kicks in and takes root in a man's mind. His behaviour becomes suddenly bizarre and he'll transform into a different man almost overnight.

I know this particular point about why men pull away might be especially difficult to stomach, as I'm sure this is something no woman wants to have to deal with. But I would most certainly be remiss if I wasn't radically honest with you about some of the uglier things men think about and deal with internally when it comes to women and dating.

7

He has a textbook psychological fear of commitment.

I'm of the strong opinion that in most cases, when a guy admits to a woman that he has "commitment issues", it's usually a ploy to win her empathy and lead her to believe thoughts like: *"Oh my! He must have been hurt before...that's why he's broken...maybe I'm the woman that can fix him!"*

No, you're not.

With that said, even though guys sometimes deceitfully play the "commitment issue" card, in a few cases, you might actually come across a man who truly has some serious anxiety issues when it comes to commitment and intimacy. And when I say serious...I mean *serious*.

Defining the Problem

When a man has a textbook psychological fear of commitment, he tends to feel and therefore emit contradicting emotions that range from a craving for love and connection to an insatiable need for complete autonomy and sexual variety. The commitment-phobic man feels an intense amount of anxiety whenever emotional intimacy is required as a relationship begins to deepen. Because of the overwhelming feelings of dread, terror, and anxiety they feel, guys like this tend to self-sabotage their relationships with women so as to avoid the apparent permanency of a serious commitment.

The big problem here is that commitment-phobic men do things, whether subconsciously or consciously, to destroy the relationship. This is not because they don't want love and connection, but partially because their fear has greater sway over their behaviour. The powerful feelings of fear and anxiety cloud their judgment, resulting in irrational anxiety-avoidant behaviours. Hence, if you find yourself dating a guy like this, once his relationship anxiety finally becomes intolerable, he will find a way to get rid of it by removing the one thing in his life that is creating the anxiety, which is YOU.

Guys like this dwell in the realm of fantasy and escapism, believing that if they could just find the right partner all their fears and worries about commitment will quickly dissolve, which would allow them to experience true love and connection. Unfortunately, for the commitment-phobic man, no partner is ever "right enough" or even "good enough." Even if they had the combined phenomenal cosmic power of Aladdin's genie and Merlin's magic to "poof" the perfect woman into their arms, they would STILL find something wrong with her to help them justify her impending and unavoidable dismissal.

Men Who Pursue Only to Withdraw

The commitment-phobic man follows a pursue-and-withdraw pattern of dating. First, he will do whatever he can to convince a woman that he desires her love and commitment more than anything. This usually lasts up until the unsuspecting female in question begins to give in to his advances. Once she begins to show a real interest and desire for commitment, Mr. Commitment-Phobe unceremoniously switches modes on her. With her heart now set on him, he starts to shut down emotionally as thoughts of being trapped, cornered, and stuck with you forever overwhelm him and dominate his mind. He then falls into a dark rabbit hole of neurotic thinking where his once endearing attitude of, *"I must have her all to myself...I want her so badly"* abruptly changes into, *"Wait...she's mine now? Good heavens! What have I done?"*

As you can see, trying to "convince" or "influence" a man like this is beyond both your jurisdiction and professional training. The fear these men experience is so intense that the issues they face can only be solved through therapy and a lot of proactive personal development. Don't expect to "fix him" by chasing him when he pulls away or by trying to hold on to him for dear life.

Also, be extra cautious of the traps a guy like this might set up in order to get you back into his life. He might do something as obvious as plead for another try if you finally dissolve the relationship, or he might attempt something a bit more subtle, like making it appear as if he wants to at least remain "friends."

Don't be fooled.

Both of these are merely the commitment-phobe's way of getting back into your life. For example, if he begs you for another chance and you take him back, he will simply repeat his pursue-and-withdraw pattern once more. And since he's much more familiar with you (since he knows how you think and what makes you tick), he'll become <u>exceedingly efficient at</u> wasting your time. The "let's be friends" angle is merely his way of sneaking back into your life without setting off his own commitment-phobia. He'll lull you into a false sense of security and, just like before, once you fall for him again he'll take you on that all familiar ride.

I should note that while there have been some notable criticisms with the whole idea of commitment-phobia I still believe it benefits a woman greatly to be well informed on the subject. You can save yourself from tons of unnecessary heartache and turmoil if you're at least able to recognize a commitment-phobic man should you so happen to come across one.

Also keep in mind that commitment-phobia isn't reserved just for the male species. Countless women struggle with this debilitating fear as well, and have abandoned or destroyed quality relationships with great guys because of it. But since this is a book *for* women *about* men, I've chosen to focus on the men to fittingly explain this point.

Chapter 3:

When Your Dating Habits

Drive Him Away

8

He thought you weren't that interested in him.

If you ask enough guys to list some of the more irritating reasons why they might lose interest and stop contacting a woman they went out with a few times, you'd soon discover that one of the most common answers is this: a lack of noticeable romantic interest on the part of the woman. For whatever reason, if a man concludes that you're just not that interested in him, **even if you actually are**, if he has a healthy amount of self-respect he'll quickly stop calling you to save himself any further embarrassment.

Now, this sort of dating situation usually occurs when there is either a *miscommunication of interest* or a *mismatch in dating expectations*. Under both of these reasons exists a plethora of unfruitful dating situations. Here are a few of the main ones that are most likely to occur:

1. You show a lack of enthusiasm on dates and in your text messages...

This might happen if you're feeling "on the fence" about a guy or if you're currently casually dating several men at once. With so many options on your plate, you might not be enthusiastic about any one particular guy, even if he's showing you a sincere and consistent level of interest.

A lack of enthusiasm from the woman we're dating is a desire killer for men. When a woman doesn't show her enthusiasm for us it turns a potentially fun dinner conversation into a boring interview and makes us feel super creepy if we attempt to initiate any kind of physical contact. It's okay to act calm and pleasantly content during the first and second dates with a guy in order to keep him from thinking you're head-over-heels infatuated with him, but by the third date you should be showing more enthusiasm while interacting with him IF you want to reassure him of your interest and keep him invested in pursuing you.

The same thing applies for how you keep in touch with him. As I mention in my book, _Texts So Good He Can't Ignore_, if your text messages come off as indifferent, overly aloof, or even too friendly (as in "friend-zoney") he might be led to believe that you don't share the same level of romantic interest that he has for you. Men are well aware of the possibility of landing in a woman's friend-zone, and most guys (if not all) have been placed there at some point in their lives. Because of the very real fear of landing in a woman's friend-zone, you'll find that some guys have developed a low tolerance policy for women who don't show enough enthusiasm. Again, if you've been out a few times and Mr. McDreamy has been clear and consistent with his interest in you, ramp up your texts with flirting, playful banter, teasing, and even offer up date suggestions so that he can clearly see that you are, in fact, _romantically_ interested in him.

2. You're lazy when it comes to attracting men and prefer men to do *all* the work...

If you once had a taste for men "below your league" or those who placed you on a pedestal, you may have developed an entitled and overly passive attitude towards dating that won't serve you well with more mature, higher status men.

I've also come across women who just don't seem to get it when it comes to the game of seduction. They either fail to make full use of their feminine allures to keep a man interested or they are simply unaware that they possess a power over men that can make us scorching hot with desire.

Don't be lazy. Utilize your feminine charms to the fullest if you truly want a man worthy of your all. Remember, men *want* to be spellbound by a woman's love just as much as women want to feel overwhelmed and enraptured by a man's passion.

3. You pretend to be hard-to-get and feign disinterest in order to stoke men's desire for you...

Playing hard-to-get (which is not the same as actually *being* hard-to-get) and feigning disinterest is an extremely hazardous seduction strategy because you run the risk of deterring higher quality men. The reason for this is because guys like this tend to maximize their dating success by only pursuing women who appear highly interested in them. Playing hard-to-get might have worked when you were younger (and perhaps on younger, less experienced men), but as you meet more experienced, higher quality men, don't expect to get the same results.

Younger and/or less experienced men sometimes fall into the humiliating habit of chasing women who show little to no interest in them. But as a man matures, meets and dates more women, and gleans lessons from those experiences, he eventually learns how to *quickly* tell if a woman is interested in him, on the fence/neutral, or uninterested.

Obviously, no man in his right mind is going to waste time on someone who is clearly disinterested. But even appearing *somewhat* interested or indifferent could work against you. We know that our time is better spent with a woman who displays sincere and enthusiastic interest than someone who appears to be "on the fence" about us.

4. He's lazy and expects *you* to do all the work and chase him...

Some guys are just as lazy and/or self-entitled as some women are when it comes to dating. If they are accustomed to having women chase and beg them for attention, when they happen to come across a high-value woman (the kind of woman who doesn't chase men), they might expect her to blindly pursue them as well. Assuming you are a high-value woman, after several interactions with you a guy like this may conclude that you're just not interested enough and that you're not worth the effort. Having a guy like this bail on you after several dates is a good thing, since he probably wasn't interested in pursuing a real relationship with you in the first place.

5. He's shy and/or lacks enough experience with women to pick up on their subtle (and not so subtle) signals of romantic interest...

Shyer men and those with less experience with

women tend to have more trouble picking up on a woman's attraction signals. If you come across guys like this, the only thing you can do is be a bit more assertive with them, preferably in a gracious way. If you conclude that he's genuinely interested in you based on his texts and behaviour, you may have to be the one to make the first few moves in terms of planning a date or inviting him out to an event with you. Just know that once you get the ball rolling, if he fails to take the lead by planning dates and initiating contact with you he may turn out to be a waste of time.

Now, keep in mind that I'm not advising you to chase a man. There's no problem with passing on guys like this if they fail to take a hint, especially if you'd prefer to be courted by a more assertive, determined, and experienced man. If you want to be pursued from the beginning, prioritize dating men who decisively go after what they want.

Follow His Lead to Show Your Interest

Here's the thing, as the prime initiators of romantic interest, men risk rejection in order to secure the desire and attention of women. Because of this, we need to feel as if the woman we've began courting is making a **noticeable investment** to move things forward in a budding romance. We *need* positive, enthusiastic, and definite feedback from her to feel reassured that our efforts are making a difference. Remember, men have feelings too, so be sure to display your interest in a way that arouses his confidence.

9

You turned him off by coming on too strong and pursuing him.

Generally, men are wired by nature to be the 'aggressors' when it comes to romantic relationships. We enjoy the *process* of discovering the true depth of a woman's value and what she could potentially mean to us in the future. Unravelling her tantalizing mysteries and dismantling the protective barriers a woman has placed around her love and affection is what maintains our interest, especially during the early phases of a romance. We go to great lengths to repeatedly test and break down a woman's boundaries until she finally submits to our insistent passion and grants us uninhibited access to her heart and more.

Unfortunately, although many women know that men want to be the pursuer when it comes to romantic relationships, they still tend to fall into the fruitless habit of coming on too strong and too fast when a new guy begins to take an interest in them. Yes, I understand the sense of urgency and necessity you feel when you come across a really phenomenal guy and you don't want him to lose interest. And I also understand the intense feelings of romantic passion that may compel you to give your heart to a man prematurely all because you genuinely want him and don't want to play games. Of course, you're somewhat justified in acting this way, as higher quality men aren't interested in game-playing either. However, don't confuse "playing games" with the idea of allowing yourself to be "thoroughly wooed" by a man.

Why Men Want and Need to Pursue You

If you remember what I said in the first paragraph you would realize that the *process* of discovering a woman's self-worth and breaking down the walls to her personal charms and pleasures plays a major role in helping us fall in love with her. At the risk of annoying you, I'm going to repeat that again: *The process of discovering a woman's self-worth and slowly breaking down the walls to her personal intimacies and pleasures plays a major role in helping us fall in love with her.* If a man is robbed of this *process* because you start coming on too strong or pursuing him, in most cases he will suddenly lose interest in you without really understanding why.

When you start pursuing him, in his mind, a man knows that the dynamic has suddenly shifted. He now realizes that he resides in a place of importance in your mind that is greater than the place of importance he holds for you. Once this has happened, the "game" is lost for you because the man in question no longer has the opportunity to experience what he *really* desires – **the conquest of a great woman's love**.

Now, I honestly believe that a good majority of women have no idea what "coming on too strong" behaviours looks like to men. This is why you might be reading this and rolling your eyes while thinking, *"Yes, I already know men want to be the pursuers and I never come on too strong, etc.…"* but do you actually know for sure what "coming on too strong" actually looks like to a guy? Well, let's find out.

Here are a few of the most common behaviours women unknowingly exhibit when they're coming on too strong or begin pursuing a man:

1. Dominating the initiations of contact – If you find yourself being the first (and sometimes only) one to text and call when dating a guy, you're making it too easy for him. Doing this tells a man that you don't have anything else better to do other than trying to get his attention, which causes your value as a long-term romantic partner to diminish in his eyes. This might be difficult for some women to swallow, but if you were to ask your most blunt and honest guy friends about it (the ones that really care about you), they'd confirm this truth.

In the early stages of a blossoming romance, if you're *always* messaging a guy back too quickly, where he's barely moved his finger away from the "SEND" button before you respond back to him, he'll *know* that he "has you", which means pursuing you passionately is **no longer a top priority** of his. Keep this in mind the next time you start dating a guy and you realize that he's rarely (if ever) the first one to initiate contact to keep in touch, flirt, or make future dating plans. If you find yourself dominating the initiations of contact in this way, you've officially become the "aggressor" in the relationship and are coming on too strong.

2. Cancelling your plans to make room for him – If you've only been on a handful of dates and this guy is clearly not even your boyfriend yet, there's absolutely no reason for you to cancel your already-made plans just to spend time with him. If he suggests a date and it really isn't convenient for you, tell him it isn't a good time and then suggest a future date.

This is a clear example of actually *being* hard-to-get and not *playing* hard-to-get. Your fun, busy life makes you attractive to men, so don't be quick to give it up just because Mr. McDreamy wants to see more of you. On some level, a man must know that you're "making room" for him in your life. This keeps him from feeling pressured to "fill in your missing pieces", since if you didn't have a fun, busy life of your own your over-eagerness to make time for him will quickly make him realize that you might become a Stage 5 Clinger after only one month of dating.

3. Heavily alluding to your sexual prowess and desires in your flirting – Depending on what it is you're really after, your mileage may vary with this advice, but I'll mention it anyway: Being overtly sexual in your flirting can potentially scare away men who are looking for a serious long-term partner. Granted, it won't scare away all guys, but a good portion of relationship-minded men will actually be turned off from this kind of behaviour.

In this scenario, what we have is a mismatch in wants. Alluding to your sexual prowess or appetites in text and conversation with a man you've only been on a handful of dates with will send him a very clear message: That you're open to casual, sexual encounters with men. If the guy in question is looking for a long-term girlfriend or even a future wife, this sort of behaviour will immediately send up a red flag that tells him (whether it's true or not) that you're promiscuous and easy-to-bed.

Again, whether you're sexually promiscuous or not doesn't matter. What matters is that when you flirt in this way, this is the message that men receive. In this case, you're coming on too strong because he may be led to believe that you're more interested in casual, sexual encounters while he's actually interested in finding his Miss Right – the woman he can confidently pursue for a long-term relationship.

4. Being overly presumptuous in regards to his interest in you – For the love of Pete, don't change your Facebook status to "In A Relationship" or "It's Complicated" after your first (second, third, or fourth) date with a guy who has yet to make you his girlfriend (or anything else for that matter). It's a clear sign that a woman is coming on a bit too strong whenever she *assumes* that a man belongs to her and thus starts acting in those all too common crazy ways that scare men off and make them never call back again.

Aside from telling the world that someone is your boyfriend/lover/complication when he's clearly not, there are a variety of other behaviours that fit this category. Such things include:

1. Inviting yourself to his place/his social events without his knowing or authorization.

2. Making inconsiderate demands of his time and/or resources that even a best friend would be hesitant to make.

3. Making unwarranted confessions of love and devotion suited best for couples in love.

4. Getting angry and insolent when he fails to show an extravagant (and undeserved) amount of

interest in you.

5. Offering him gifts and trinkets that are clearly in the domain of "boyfriend-girlfriend" type gifts, and lastly…

6. Lavishing him with lovey-dovey public displays of affection to make it seem as if he belongs to you.

While some women might think that such behaviour is actually kind of "sweet", don't be misled. If a guy is just getting to know you (and is therefore quietly appraising your true value and self-worth) don't make him think you're desperate for him by exhibiting any of the behaviours I've listed above.

5. Exhibiting inauthentic or ingratiating behaviour – No matter how "dreamy" or out-of-your-league you think a guy is because of his looks or social status, if you want him to take you seriously you must refrain from grovelling and acting fake just to please him. These sorts of behaviours include: lying about yourself to win his approval, dumbing down your intelligence, acting more intelligent/well-read/educated than you really are, pretending to like the things he likes, stretching yourself thin to prove your value as a girlfriend, etc.

The thing is, such behaviour might actually be the worst of the "coming on too strong" behaviours I've mentioned because it is a clear sign that a woman values more the approval and valuations of the man she's interested in rather than her own. This sort of behaviour screams 'desperate' and drives away those guys who are most interested in finding a long-term girlfriend. The only kind of guys who will stick around are opportunistic men who enjoy exploiting a woman's low self-esteem to get their own needs met, which usually comes at the expense of a woman's dignity. Try to keep this in mind if you find yourself tempted to act in an insincere manner in hopes that it might keep a man around for the long-term.

6. Revealing too much information about yourself way too early – While we can't help but talk a bit much about ourselves when we're *really* interested in someone, there is a fine line between *sharing* who you are with someone and *shoving* who you are down their throat. If you've been dating less than a month, why should a guy know the odd inner machinations of your particular menstrual cycle? Why does he need to know about the time you caught your ex-boyfriend cheating on you and how you smashed his windshield in a moment of white-hot rage?

Believe me when I say that information like this is better saved for boyfriends who are already *familiar* with you or guys who are extremely close to being boyfriends. But in some cases, certain types of information are just better kept to yourself, especially if they involve youthful indiscretions of which you're not particularly proud.

At the end of the day, knowing what to reveal and what not to reveal should come down to simple common sense and social etiquette. For example, if you're out on a fourth date and a guy offers you peanuts, saying, *"No thanks, I'm actually allergic. I'll swell up like the Michelin Man if I have even just one"*, is perfectly fine and even kind of funny. On the other hand, randomly informing a guy that ice cream gives you extra gross, butt-leaky diarrhoea is far too much information, especially if what you're doing has absolutely nothing to do with ice cream at all. I mean, even if you are doing something where ice cream is offered to you, a simple, *"No thanks, I'm lactose intolerant"*, is a thousand times more palatable to the average man's ears.

Being diplomatic and displaying common etiquette is important for all types of relationships. So even though you may be in a hurry to quickly close the gap of unfamiliarity between you and Mr. Tall-Dark-and-Handsome, don't scare him off by offering unsolicited (and usually unattractive) information about yourself.

7. Questioning him about how little he keeps in touch with you – Don't question a man about how little he texts or calls you, especially earlier on in a new romance. Sure, as a relationship develops and he becomes your boyfriend you could openly express your concerns about his poor communication habits, but before such a relationship has been established it is better to just let him be. Instead of asking a new potential beau why he hasn't called you, etc., simply ignore him and again, fill your life with interesting activities with interesting people (including other men). In fact, the more interesting activities and interesting people you have in your life the *easier* it will be for you to forget the fact that he hasn't called you in a week.

8. Stalking him on social media – While communicating through Facebook's private messaging is a great way to keep in touch and cultivate interest with a guy, liking his posts, liking his pictures, replying to his posts, and commenting on his pictures, etc., will make you appear as if you're trying too hard to win his approval. Even though he might be flattered that you 'liked' his profile picture and commented on his latest

Instagram, over time he'll start getting creeped out if you keep finding new ways to merge your online life with his own.

9. Making desperate little attempts to remind him that you still exist – If a man hasn't called or texted you in a while or when you *think* he should have, resist the temptation to remind him that you "still exist." Texting him a random little, *"Hey, what's up?"* or sending him a winky emoji won't make him contact you (or fall in love with you) any faster. In fact, the reverse is likely to happen. It's even worse if you decide to show up to his apartment/work/gym/regular hangout spot unannounced. Behaviours like this scream "desperation" and the more experienced and opportunistic a man is, the more likely he is to capitalize on your obvious obsession with him.

The Rare Exception

Now, I do have one confession in regards to this overall topic. The more attracted to and interested in you a guy is, the more tolerant he will be towards any behaviour that makes it seem as if you're "coming on too strong." If he finds something special about you that he hasn't come across in any other woman (this can be anything from your physical beauty to shared interests) he is more likely to overlook a certain level of "needy" or overly infatuated behaviour so long as such behaviour doesn't overshadow the level of interest he has in you.

This is great news for the single and searching woman simply because she doesn't have to become excessively cautious in regards to how she regulates her dating behaviour. For example, if a guy finds you irresistible from the first date, he's less likely to care if you messaged him early the next day to say you had a fabulous time or if you revealed just a tad bit more about yourself than you know you should have while on the date. But do keep in mind that such cases are the exceptions…not the rule. Considering both the law of averages and the norm expectations of male behaviour, the women who *will* experience the most dating success will still put a lot of effort into ensuring that they're not broadcasting desperation and unmerited devotedness to a man by coming on too strong.

10

You became totally devoted to him prematurely after mistaking his infatuation as a sign of his capacity to commit.

Tread very carefully when a man pursues you passionately and makes bold claims about his love for or adoration of you, especially if he's only been dating you two months or less and doesn't REALLY know the real you (you know, the sometimes insecure, unreasonable, but lovable YOU).

On your journey to find Mr. Right, you may come across a man who will pursue you with extraordinary romantic passion, make you believe he'd lasso the moon out of the night sky for you, and maybe even insist that you cease from seeing other men and date him exclusively. Then, once his seduction has proved successful and you begin to seriously fall for him...he loses interest, pulls away, and eventually disappears without so much as an explanation. But why does this happen?

Well, if things were going along swimmingly prior to you becoming devoted to a guy like this and making yourself more available to him, you might deduce that he was only after the thrill of chasing you. In some cases, this is true. But this isn't necessarily the most common reason why men pull away in these situations. When a man goes all out during the early dating stages then suddenly loses interest and pulls away once you start to reciprocate his "passion intensity", it's either because:

1. He really wasn't that interested in you in the first place, or...

2. Your "passion intensity" (at least, your version of it) scared him off.

Let's look at both of these situations in a bit more depth.

Are You Scaring Him Away?

Now, if we consider the former, where he really wasn't that interested in you to begin with, then you've actually lost nothing. In situations like this there's really nothing a woman can do except to maintain her dignity and force herself not to chase the withdrawing man. If he pursued you with the utmost passion and has begun to slide away now that you've started reciprocating his interest, simply cease contacting him and wait for him to come to you and prove himself a reliable suitor.

If he does begin pursuing you again, follow his lead and simply focus on reciprocating his acts of romantic interest. Doing so will allow you to effectively gauge his true interest and capacity to commit to you over time. You must not fall into the ugly game of Chase-a-Man in such cases, as it will wreak havoc on your self-esteem while ultimately increasing his own in the process. Read that last sentence again.

Now, if it was the latter, where your "passion intensity" scared him off, that's another issue altogether. Your "passion intensity" is basically the behavior you exhibit once you've fallen for a guy. It's the things you say (and stop saying) and the things you do (and stop doing) once you've been convinced that a man is "for real" and worth your time, attention, love, and emotional investment. While I honestly believe that the right guy will appreciate your unique brand of love and devotion and will not take it for granted, I've dated enough women and have heard the dating stories of many more to know for certain that a lot of women have no idea that their "passion intensity", no matter how genuine, makes them appear aggressive and emotionally overwhelming, and therefore at times…*unattractive*. And as the less emotionally intuitive of the genders, although men can't always immediately specify when a woman begins to give off this unattractive "low value" vibe, when it does happen, we can *feel* it.

Here's how this plays out for a well-meaning guy (let's call him Brad).

Brad has just begun dating Linda, and he really, really likes her. In fact, he's never felt this way about any woman before, and **genuinely feels** as if she might be the girl for him. So naturally, feeling this way, Brad wants to convince her that he's the real deal. But after about two and a half months of vigorous dating, Brad begins to pull away from Linda, after realizing that she's...changed.

At this point in the romance, Linda has seemingly become less fun and spontaneous as she now wants to plan every date ahead of schedule. She begins to hang out with her friends less and suddenly wants to accompany Brad to many of his functions as she *invites herself* along. Their once fun and laid-back conversations become bland and serious as Linda spends time idealizing about the future *while complaining about the present*.

She suddenly starts to call Brad WAY more than he calls her, and it takes him an entire lunch break to catch up with all of her "cute" text messages. Linda also becomes jealous or testy when Brad wants to do the things he used to already do before he met her; things like hanging out with his friends, going to the gym four times a week, or working overtime on Saturdays to get ahead in his career.

Of course, Linda isn't doing this because she's selfish or manipulative. She really just loves Brad and wants to spend more time with him. Naturally, because Brad shows resistance to Linda's change in behavior, Linda pursues him even more as fears of losing him flood her mind. This only makes things worse as Brad becomes more and more disheartened. He *wants* to continue dating Linda but he doesn't *feel* that overwhelming pull towards her anymore.

Even worse, Brad just can't seem to understand what's happening. According to him, he did all the right things. He called her often, actually took her out on real dates, and even introduced her to his friends and family. He did all these things with the hopes that *this* girl was different, that *this* girl had that certain special something, and that *this* girl was worth pursuing. As he loses interest, Brad pulls away and feels both dejected and embarrassed about it because he already told everyone how much this girl meant to him. Brad eventually disappears without an explanation, as he simply doesn't know what happened or how to fix it, and unfortunately...neither does Linda.

When Your Natural Drives Dictate How You Date

If you've experienced anything even remotely similar to Linda, I feel for you. However, I'm not a woman and therefore have no idea what it *really* feels like when you've finally set your heart on a man and give him your all only to have him lose interest. But even though my ability to empathize may be limited, perhaps I can shed some light on such situations from Brad's perspective.

Here's the thing. Women, in general, tend to have a strong urge to want to *absorb* themselves into a man's life so that "the two become one." While this is a beautiful part of being female, you have to consider what this behavior looks like to a man **when it is not kept in check or tempered with seductive womanly subtlety**. Without a good amount of experience with men and dating, many women have no idea that they're allowing their primal mating drives to dictate their behavior. Because of this, they end up prematurely devoting themselves to men who might be romantically sincere but ultimately unproven.

Now, you may be thinking, *"Well, if this is all a part of being a woman and this is who I am, then there's nothing wrong with being this way. I'm sure there's some guy out there that…"* let me just stop that train of thought right there. I'm convinced that allowing your natural feminine drives to completely dictate your dating behavior is the number one, underlying reason why women fail with men.

The thing is, the act of attracting a man and keeping him interested in you long enough to commit for the long-term requires tact, subtlety, and most importantly, feminine seduction. Thus, when your "passion intensity" becomes masculine and/or manipulative (like Linda's behaviors), it immediately turns men off, especially men who revel in their masculinity.

Aggressive attempts to merge your life with his, getting jealous or cantankerous when he's not spending time with you, and dominating the initiation of contact are controlling behaviors that make men feel as if they've lost something when a woman begins to behave like this. Men can't quite put their finger on it, but when a woman's "passion intensity" isn't tempered with both her own self-respect (like the undignified things you won't do to keep him around) AND respect for the needs of the masculine heart (like his need for a great romantic conquest, to be seduced into a commitment, to convince a high-value woman of <u>his</u> worth, etc.) their once beautiful, high-value woman suddenly seems a little less polished and a whole less feminine, and therefore less attractive. Such behavior repels men and causes them to reject you and whatever relationship you did possess all because you went from being the one pursued to unknowingly becoming the pursuer.

Don't keep making the mistake of thinking that a man's romantic intensity is of the same nature as your own. In most cases, it is not, and convincing yourself otherwise is the fastest way to disappointment and heartache once you realize that he was nowhere near as interested in a committed relationship with you as you had assumed.

So what's the big takeaway here? It's simple really: When you find yourself falling for a particular guy and you want to reciprocate his devotion, be willing to show your own devotion but always do so with dignity and a little restraint. Let him lead and simply **reciprocate his investment** in your own unique way. When he takes a step toward you, take a step toward him by accepting him graciously and letting him experience more of your world and your love. When he takes two steps toward you, you can then take more initiative by making a big step toward him. Simply continue to match his pace and reciprocate his level of investment in the relationship with your own offers of love and romance.

Remember, discretion and self-control are key when cultivating a relationship with a man, as he needs to feel as if *he's* the one doing the "conquering." Yes, you're doing your own version of "romantic conquering", but as a woman, your dating strategy is most successful when it is passive, reluctant, and respectful of the masculine heart. Behaving in this way is the most effective method for reciprocating a man's insistent passions without succumbing to the anxious, obsessive, aggressive, and even masculine behaviors that cause women to unknowingly turn men off for good.

11

He couldn't cultivate or maintain a deep romantic connection to you because of your "masculine" interpersonal behaviors.

While this might be an issue for a wide variety of women, it seems as if this particular dating dilemma is an on-going struggle for highly intelligent, accomplished, financially successful, and high-status women in their forties and older. Many women in this demographic, due to their cumulative life experiences and education, have adopted very masculine and self-interested attitudes that have helped them to get ahead in their careers and businesses. Unfortunately, because highly masculine men generally prefer dating highly feminine women, these masculine interpersonal behaviours tend to turn men off, especially in the earlier dating stages.

In the beginning stages, men tend to be very judicious about a woman's behaviour. Men are very sensitive to things like bossiness, high-maintenance, self-entitlement (gold-digging), and self-absorption (overly career-oriented, lifestyle obsessed, or accomplishment focused), and tend to dismiss women after these behaviours reveal themselves within those first few weeks of dating. The fact is, what men really want to experience when they're with a woman is her passion, kindness, compassion, tenderness, sensuality, nurturing, patience, dignity, and fidelity. These are all the heart-focused and <u>emotional</u> characteristics that make men fall in love with a woman during every encounter with her; the very same feminine qualities that quickly captures a man's heart.

So what's the solution to this particular dating dilemma? Simple. Present yourself in a more feminine light, let men pursue you, and learn to "let your hair down" whenever you're interacting with a romantic prospect.

The Art of "Letting Your Hair Down" Around Men

Start off by figuring out exactly where you fall on the sliding scale of masculine vs. feminine behaviours whenever you interact with men, and then make a concentrated effort to inject a bit more feminine grace in your behaviour and communication. If you've read any of my other books (and shame on you if you haven't), I don't think I have to explain the obvious reasons why masculine men are helplessly attracted to unapologetically feminine women. Instead of lamenting that men should "man up" and be able to handle you regardless of how you present yourself, put the odds in your favour by accepting men *as they presently are* (and have been for thousands of years) and adjust the way you interact with them.

Believe me, this is much simpler than it sounds.

Think of it this way. Most of the things you find attractive about a guy, his intelligence, his ambition, his sense of humour, his worldly experience, his success and accomplishments, etc., aren't necessarily the things he's most attracted to in you. Not at the outset at least. Instead, men are much more interested in experiencing your "feminine energy", or simply, your enthusiasm, your playfulness, your sensitivity, your cheerfulness, your gentleness, your relationship with your family, your passions, your modesty and willingness to let them provide and protect you in small ways, your ability to empathize with others, your level of politeness, kindness, and thoughtfulness towards others, etc., which are all things they pick up in your body language as well as the way you speak and how you interact with them *and* other people. In other words, men want to *feel* a romantic connection to you, and don't care so much about making an intellectual connection right at the beginning. Read that last sentence again.

The good thing is that you don't always have to be "more" feminine to attract men per se. You just need to know how to tap into your own natural level of femininity when you're interacting with them. How you interact with men on the job or in your business won't get you the romance you want. You have to learn how to "let your hair down" around the guys you're interested in if you want them to see you as a romantic prospect as opposed to "just a friend."

Keep Him Coming Back with Your Feminine Energy

If you've been very career-focused or blissfully single for a long time, you might have unknowingly built a wall of "competing interests" around yourself in which the guys you date are forced to work twice as hard just to spend some time with you. While a highly interested guy doesn't mind putting in the work to win your heart, he probably doesn't want to overextend himself doing so and thus, end up feeling as if he's making a fool of himself in the process. Ultimately, men (especially older men) don't want to have to compete with your career, friends, travel plans, social causes, etc., as **they'd rather be with a woman who recognizes their value just as much as they recognize hers**. The feminine approach, therefore, is to be receptive, responsive, interested, and appreciative, while allowing him the gift of pursuing you.

Another way your behaviour might come off as masculine or overly self-interested is through how aggressive you are about "moving things forward" or getting your way with a guy. In regards to your desire to move things forward as quickly as possible, you must remember that in romantic relationships, most men like to *feel* like the pursuers. The moment a guy realizes you're chasing him or that you're hell-bent on securing a commitment, he'll begin to lose interest. Instead of being aggressive in your pursuit, relax into your femininity and simply reciprocate his investment. Let him do *most* of the initiating of contact, especially in the beginning, and allow him to make plans and set the course of the relationship. While there are things a woman can do to "nudge" things forward a bit, for the most part, at least in the beginning, most men will want to do the pursuing.

Whenever he takes a step toward you in earnest, reciprocate his investment by **showing your appreciation**, illustrating your interest in him, and being open and receptive to his acts of love and kindness. Flirt with him when he's not around via texting (if he's so inclined to receive texts), hint that you enjoy his company and would be open to seeing more of him (on real dates, of course), and give him the space he needs to miss you. In short, lean back and let him pursue you, as a man is more likely to fall in love with a woman who demonstrates that while she deeply desires him, she has no interest in controlling him. Read that last sentence again.

In regards to getting your way with men, this might be challenging for you if you're quite accustomed to getting your way in other areas of your life. As I pointed out in the beginning of this point, women in their forties and older might struggle with this the most, especially due to the complications that arise from dating men within their age bracket.

You see, the benefit of dating a man in his forties and beyond is that he's had time to grow in life experience and maturity. The downside of dating a man in this demographic is that the more life experience and maturity he has, the more set in his ways he might be. At this stage in his life, he'll have well-developed habits and pastimes, friends with whom he's accustomed to spending time with, a career that calls for a lot of responsibility (and thus, attention), and most importantly, family that he's fond of spending time with or responsible for taking care of, such as children or an aging parent. Naturally, at this age you'll have some, if not all of these things in your life as well. The conflict, however, occurs when the two lives meet and everyday responsibilities start to compete with your blossoming relationship.

In these situations, you have to be extremely understanding of his position in life (and ensure that he is of yours as well). Refrain from guilt-tripping him if you find that he struggles to divide his time between you and his responsibilities. Be sure you pick your battles carefully in these instances, because in the early dating stages, men are very sensitive towards having to change some vital aspect of their lives just to make a woman happy. Understanding, empathy, compassion, and honest, gracious communication are key in these situations.

For example, if a man has a grown son who is visiting him for the weekend, one who lives across the country and he hasn't seen in a year or so, don't lose your poise or become frantic if he has to change plans on you to spend some time with his son. Try to be a little flexible and avoid using passive-aggression to make him feel worse than he probably already does. Believe me, if your gentleman caller is really hooked on you and wants to make you happy, he'll feel terrible for having to change plans on you like this. In these situations, the woman who wins is the compassionate, understanding one. By giving him the guilt-free space he needs to do what he wants to do, you will make him feel as if you "get him", which will melt his heart and make him even more determined to keep you in his life.

A Different Approach for Finding Mr. Right

Interestingly, it seems as if some women who struggle to "act more feminine" with the men they're romantically interested in sometimes have better results by changing their taste in men rather than their behaviour. Highly successful, intelligent, and accomplished women are naturally attracted to higher status men who are also very successful, intelligent, and accomplished as well. Naturally, if these men are considered "alphas" on any level, they will be more attracted to women who won't compete with them for the "alpha" position in the relationship.

Instead of trying to change their behaviours from masculine to feminine, some highly successful, intelligent, and accomplished women have simply opted to date men who aren't as assertive and dominant as themselves. These men bring a different dynamic to the relationship in that they're often more naturally thoughtful, affectionate, considerate, empathic, etc., than the women they're with. This allows these "alpha" women to maintain their masculine energies in the relationship, which means everyone ends up happy. While this isn't a path that will appeal to most women, this could possibly be an avenue to explore if you constantly struggle with trying to attract and maintain the romantic interest of "alpha" types of men.

Chapter 4:

When He's Just Not Buying Whatever You're Selling

12

He didn't feel enough chemistry.

Here's the reality. A man may find you physically attractive enough to ask you out a few times but then quickly realize that he didn't feel any chemistry with you. Although chemistry (or a lack of it) is usually sensed by both parties involved, there are those occasions when one person feels a spark but the other person doesn't. In situations like this, a woman might quickly develop feelings for a man for a myriad of reasons and want to see more of him. But unfortunately, the gentleman in question doesn't feel the same and simply decided to move on without any kind of verbal or written indication that he was no longer interested.

When a guy takes you out on a handful of dates and disappears because of a lack of chemistry, consider yourself fortunate. I know, I know. Having someone ghost on you is disrespectful, humiliating, and anxiety inducing. I'm not asking you to *not* take it personally or be irritated; I'm just saying that it's better to know early on that a man wasn't that interested or attracted to you enough than to be strung along for several months of dating.

When a Guy Friend Sparks Your Interest

You may already be friends with a guy you're really

interested in and it always appears as if you're oh-so-close to getting him to make a move on you. Except he never does. He's always eager to hang out with you, is thoughtful of you, and even shares secrets with you, but ultimately…you're just a friend.

Whenever you find yourself effectively "friend-zoned" by a man who never picks up (or ignores) your romantic signals, what we have is a guy who doesn't feel any sexual chemistry with you. Sure, he might love spending time with you, adores your personality, and even acts as if you're the most fun person he's ever met, but without sexual chemistry he will continue to ignore your attempts to launch the relationship in a more romantic direction.

How do I know? Well, because on several occasions I've been the guy in this sort of situation. I've always been a pretty friendly guy, especially with the ladies, and didn't find it difficult to form friendships with the opposite sex. If I didn't feel any kind of physical attraction or sexual chemistry with a close female friend from the beginning the friendship, I most certainly didn't feel it later on. I'm not saying this is the same for *all* men, but generally, men don't take very long at all to figure out if they're romantically attracted to a woman or not.

Don't Become Firewood for His Ego

The biggest danger for a woman in any of the above situations is to find herself deeply attracted to a man who has become addicted to her attention, even though he doesn't feel any sexual chemistry. This is why I mentioned earlier that it's better to have a guy who doesn't feel that spark bail on you after several dates. If he decides to continue seeing you out of sheer boredom or because he doesn't have other dating options, he may feed into your false hope that there could ever be something serious between the two of you.

This particular danger is even more prevalent for the "friend-zoned" woman because the guy in question might not even be aware that he's using her to feed his ego. Men like attention too, and it's very tempting for a man to keep a woman close by, even if only platonically, if he knows that she's only one soft whisper away from being his. The mere idea that she's desperate for him is a major confidence booster, and he'll consistently parlay that confidence into the pursuit of *other* women. You've been warned.

13

You didn't meet his expectations.

Whether a man writes them down or not, he has a list of dating deal breakers that helps him determine if a woman is worth his commitment and long-term emotional investment. Naturally, if you in some way fail to measure up to his expectations, the man in question will ultimately lose interest in you and make an exit.

I'm sure we can agree that there's nothing wrong with a man having a list of things he wants and more importantly, requires in the woman he truly wants for a relationship. Having a list of qualities and deal breakers means that a man is at least somewhat proactive about finding a good woman to someday build a life with, and guys like this tend to approach the pursuit of a long-term mate very seriously. While this is a good thing, the problem exists when the guy you're dating eventually realizes that you don't measure up to his list or expectations but he neglects to *inform* you of his recent discovery. Instead of being upfront with you and letting you know what happened, he just suddenly disappears without a trace or an explanation.

For situations like this, we need to simplify things a bit more. It's almost impossible to list all of the various things a woman might do to turn a man off since a lot of these things will be different for each man. With this in mind, instead of focusing on what you did or said to make him disappear, it's better to focus on *why he neglected to inform you* that it WAS something you did or said.

Let me give you a personal example...

The Silent Dismissal – Going "Ghost" On a Bad Investment

There was once a young lady (we'll call her Ashley) whom I had spent several weeks communicating with back and forth. We had been good acquaintances in college, but had never really taken a romantic interest in one another until we were both finished school and joined the workforce. She was working overseas for an embassy in another country at the time. Even though we hadn't had a chance to date in person yet, we were looking forward to it. Our interest in one another was quite clear and mutual, as we flirted and kept in touch consistently over several weeks.

Things seemed to be going great, and I had high hopes for this blossoming romance as she was very attractive, intelligent, witty, and we shared many similar interests. But then, after a certain discussion with a close mutual friend of ours, I was immediately turned off from her and began ignoring her messages…indefinitely.

Now, before you set out after me with torches and pitchforks, let me explain what happened.

This mutual friend of ours was one of my closest friends, a guy I had known since kindergarten. He was the most socially connected and outgoing guy in our group of friends, and being good friends for so long, we relied on each other for impartial input when it came to the opposite sex.

One night, we were hanging out at a pool hall, and because I knew that he was familiar with Ashley as well, I told him that I'd taken an interest in her and couldn't wait to see her when she came back in town. This guy friend stopped what he was doing, looked at me with widened eyes, chuckled and shook his head right before saying something to this effect: *You do know that my cousin Gary had sex with her right? Like…all the time! Heck, even while he had a girlfriend Ashley would still beg him to let her come over and…*

I hope you see where this was going.

First of all, a major dating deal breaker of mine was that any woman I chose to pursue for a long-term relationship would not have been physical intimate with any one of my friends or even anyone within our social circle for that matter. This was an ironclad deal breaker that I would not, and could not compromise on.

84

His cousin, Gary, used to hang out with us every now and then a few years prior, so I knew Gary well enough to determine that I didn't want to date someone who had once been Gary's plaything. The mere idea of it was nauseating. Judge me if you want, but I can guarantee you that this is a common deal breaker for most men, especially highly discerning men who aren't desperate to settle down with just any willing-bodied woman.

Aside from not being able to look myself in the mirror every day, pursuing Ashley any further would have also made me an easy target for jokes and scorn among my guy friends. So what did I do? Well, I'll tell you what I *didn't* do. I sure didn't return her messages. And I sure didn't acknowledge any plans to meet with her whenever she flew back in town.

Eventually though, I'm pretty sure she took a hint and moved on. Although she probably has no idea what happened, I believe I made the right decision. Still, we can argue that I probably could have handled the situation a lot better, but keep in mind that I was younger and a lot less mature at the time. It also didn't help that the thought of dating someone who had previously been with Gary made my stomach churn.

The thing is, if I had continued to keep in touch with her any further and we had progressed into dating, it would not have lasted. As I already mentioned, I was dating for something serious, and with the information I now knew about Ashley I would *never* be able to convince myself to take her seriously. If I had continued to see her, I would have only wasted my time and hers. I would have fallen into old habits and would have used her to "pass the time" until another woman (one not sexually acquainted with my social group) came along.

Hence, by making a *hasty* exit out of her life, I actually did her a favour.

Could I have at least informed her that I was no longer interested? Sure, but why even bother with such an awkward encounter when she would have surely requested an explanation. Based on the nature of why I lost interest in her, I'm sure you can agree with me that it was quite unnecessary for me to inform this young lady as to why I no longer wanted to pursue her. Can you imagine that conversation? I can't.

Now, with my little tale in mind, you must consider that sometimes a man will call things off and stop pursuing you when he realizes that something about you makes you an incompatible match for him. It could be something as petty as the fact that he can't stand the way you chew or something more serious, such as your religious differences. Regardless of what the reason might be, the best approach for getting past these situations with your sanity intact is to simply accept the reality that you're not going to be "The One" for every single man you come across.

Why Men Lie About or Don't Explain Their Loss of Interest

Assuming the guy in question has a high level of class, actually cares about you, and wants to let you down easy, one thing I can admit is that the less petty, superficial, niggling, "sexist", or embarrassing a deal breaker or turn off is for him, the more likely he is to inform you about it, especially if you ask him for an explanation. If it's something huge like you living six hours away from him, your religious differences, or even him being relocated because of his career, men usually don't have any qualms discussing such things because these sorts of deal breakers are reasonable, and in some cases, can be worked around if both parties are willing. However, if the deal breaker or turn off is something a bit more personal or seemingly superficial, you probably won't get an explanation for his loss of interest and eventual ghosting.

For example, a guy might not tell you that your snorting laughter drove him nuts. He might tell his friends, however, but don't count on him telling you because it might make him sound shallow. A guy isn't going to tell you that although the chemistry was crazy on your first date, when you both met up for a second date your breath made his eyes water (because of the extra spicy, garlic-infused chips you were snacking on all day). Most men aren't going to tell you that even though they endured the first date out of courtesy, they quickly lost interest after realizing you looked a lot less flattering in person when compared to the picture on your online dating profile. Most men aren't going to tell you that they thought you were fun and irresistible until you showed them your insane taxidermy collection. Most men aren't going to tell you that they were "in love" with you until you accidently forgot to flush the toilet when you came by for a dinner date. And most men aren't going to tell you that you were absolutely "The One" right up until you told him that your favourite pastimes were "sleeping and eating."

Now, please don't hate the messenger. I'm just telling you what men sometimes talk about amongst themselves after they stop seeing a woman. In cases where something seemingly superficial turns a man off of you, consider yourself fortunate if he loses interest earlier than later. Because so long as this superficial quality isn't commonly considered a red flag by the majority of the male population, you'll eventually find at least one man who LOVES your particular brand of quirkiness and who's so attracted to you that your mistakes will hardly make a difference to him.

Believe me, men *can* be superficial and shallow at times, but when a man is looking for a long-term girlfriend or even a potential wife, he wants to ensure that the things he finds annoying about his woman are things he can live with. So long as a man isn't being unreasonable, this is a smart way to go about selecting a long-term mate.

Remember, before a man really knows you his romantic obsessions with you are primarily based on sexual attraction. This sexual attraction creates a powerful, hormone-infused "love fog" that will keep him somewhat blinded to who you really are at the moment. Because of this, it will take him a while before he can effectively assess your true long-term relationship compatibility with him and importance to him. A lot of guys are not aware of this, and thus they tend to make premature assumptions and declarations regarding their capacity and ability to commit to you. This is why a man can passionately pursue you in the early dating stages and suddenly (or slowly) pull away once he gets to know the real you and realizes that you're not *his* kind of relationship material.

Therefore, if you keep in mind that men are more prone to errors in judgment regarding their true level of interest and commitment to a woman during the early dating stages, you're less likely to fall for a man's premature pledges of love and loyalty.

What Scares Men Away on a First Date

Another huge struggle for many women is when men don't call back or ask for another rendezvous after a seemingly great first date. According to the research done by Rachel Greenwald, author of the book, *Have Him at Hello: Confessions from 1,000 Guys About What Makes Them Fall in Love...Or Never Call Back*, the number one reason why the men she interviewed said that they *didn't* call a woman back for another date was simply because she was too "bossy." After interviewing over one-thousand men about the things that increased their desire to see a woman again (or not), their comments about the "Boss Lady" kept surprising her and gave her an eye-opening view into how men observe and appraise female behaviour, especially when it came to first impressions.

In her book, she reveals that the "Boss Lady" [2] was simply a title that men gave to women who were argumentative, competitive, controlling, not feminine, too independent, and not nurturing. On their dates with these women, the guys would admit to feeling an almost immediate loss of attraction whenever these dominant behaviours revealed themselves (this parallels the issue I discussed in point #11).

Greenwald stated that these dominant behaviours fell into the aforementioned six categories, and that the men in her study admitted that the "bossy" women they dated and didn't call back had some combination of these traits.

Here's a quick look at these behaviours and what they might look like through the eyes and experiences of a man:

89

Argumentative

- Trying to prove that you're smarter than him by escalating a simple discussion into a combative debate. (Men want intellectual conversations with a woman to be fun and refreshing, rather than combative and heated.)

- Disagreeing with him about his choices, preferences, and desires. (For example, if you're on a date and you realize he's a Paleo fanatic, there's really no need to argue with him and to try convince him otherwise just because you feel guilty about enjoying that big bowl of breadsticks the waiter just brought. Eat, be merry, and let the poor guy be.)

Competitive

- Trying to prove you're better than him by destroying him in something that was supposed to have been fun. (This won't apply to all men, but there are a lot of guys who won't take well to losing badly, whether their competitor be male or female. If you really like the guy, it's just a date, so have fun and maybe take it easy on him. If you've been bowling with your Dad since you were a kid, take it easy on Mr. Doesn't-Even-Own-His-Own-Bowling-Ball. You don't have to let him win (although it doesn't hurt), but you don't have to grandstand and rub it in either when you do win. No guy wants to hear, *"Ha! In your face! Hahaha! Man, do you suck at this!"*, after getting his butt kicked on a first date *by* his date.)

- Trying to get your way rather than finding a win-

win solution. (This sort of behaviour reveals itself in the most mundane, everyday ways, such as when making plans to see each other. If you guys are trying to engineer the most ideal way to meet up for a rendezvous, don't lead him to believe you're difficult to get along with just because you'd rather he followed *your* proposal for meeting up rather than settling on a plan that also accommodates his needs. So long as it's reasonable, try to meet him in the middle.)

- Having to win every argument rather than disagreeing graciously. (Greenwald gave a great example of a guy at a dinner party with a potential girlfriend. While he admitted that she had "potential", he lost interest in her when she got into a heated political debate with another guy at the dinner party. It wasn't that he didn't admire her passion (he did), it was the fact that she seemed more interested in "being right" and proving her adversary wrong as opposed to sharing her ideas in a gracious manner.)

Controlling

- Subtle, "helpful" comments that make you seem more like an overbearing mother or bossy older sister. (Example: "No, you're doing it wrong. Let me do it." Or, "I don't want to sit here, let's go over there." Or, "You shouldn't take that route, we'll never get there in time." Etc. Now, some of these statements are *okay* as isolated incidents, but when they begin to pile up on a single outing however, a man will see them as huge red flags. No man wants to take instructions on a date. He gets that every day on his job from his boss, or if he's in business, from his clients or customers.)

- Preferring he does things a certain way, *your way*, rather than being appreciative of him doing it in the first place.

Not Feminine

- Dressing in a way that makes you seem more like a co-worker, business prospect, or someone he might want to hire to run his company or manage his department.

- Appearing cold and professional rather than warm and welcoming on a date. (This could include anything from not flirting with him, having a masculine alpha male stride, using "business lingo" during conversation, or even talking too much about your work and career.)

Too Independent

- Not accepting his gentlemanly help when he offers it. (If he opens a door for you, let him do it and appreciate the heck out of it. If you really want to charm him, make a big deal of it and let him know how chivalrous and gallant he is and how you find men like him irresistibly attractive. You won't regret this!)

- Not accepting or responding positively to his offers to protect you, provide for you, or "possess" you in some way. (While walking the sidewalk, if he asks you to walk on the left of him so that he is closer to the oncoming traffic, don't fight him on it or make a big scene about being fully capable of walking where you want. If he offers to pay for tickets or dinner for the evening, let him do so and show your appreciation. If he suggests you try a food, beverage, or venue, be appreciative and acquiescent (naturally, if you have a valid reason to oppose his suggestion, simply ensure that you do so graciously). If he speaks up for you or defends you, don't reprimand him about how you're perfectly capable of defending yourself. He's just being protective and wants to shield you from confrontation.)

Not Nurturing

- Appearing hostile towards or completely uninterested in children or having them. (This one will be subjective, because some men aren't interested in having children either. That being said, it's still prudent to err on the side of caution when it comes to the subject of kids earlier on. Some guys are indifferent to having children and can easily swing one way or another. If you're too adamant about the kids issue way too early, you might scare him off before he's had a chance to fall in love with you and see things from your point of view.)

- Being apathetic, aloof, or harsh towards the needs of other people, children, and even animals. (Interestingly, Greenwald gave a fascinating example of a guy losing interest in a woman after she had invited him over to her apartment. Apparently, she had a puppy who, to him at least, seemed uncared for and unnoticed.

Even after the poor thing wandered over, she took a while to introduce him and even did so with a dismissive tone. It probably didn't help her case when he also noticed an empty dog bowl nearby. Sad.)

Naturally, women who unknowingly exhibit these behaviours are often confused when they learn that men view them as being very "masculine", and thus, unattractive. The problem is that women in today's highly competitive modern world have adopted these traits because they have been proven as valuable assets in helping them get ahead in their careers and businesses. This is the reason why the men in this study admitted that while they were impressed with these women, **they didn't feel any attraction to them**, and instead they often saw them as phenomenal individuals that they'd rather hire, work for, or do business with than date.

Unfortunately, these dominant traits do not translate well when it comes to interacting with men in a romantic setting, especially during the early dating stages when a guy hasn't gotten to know the *real* you yet. When a man is marriage-minded and is looking for someone he can spend his life with, he becomes a lot more discriminating throughout the dating process, especially earlier on. Guys like this don't want to waste your time or their own, and thus are very sensitive to any behaviours that might make a woman seem like an incompatible long-term partner or a bad wife and mother.

In all fairness, no woman is competitive, controlling, etc., ALL of the time. I'm pretty sure that if these guys hung around just a little longer they might have realized that the dominant behaviours they first noticed were just a small sliver of these women's personalities. Many of these women were also perhaps kind, warm, loving, nurturing, easy-going, appreciative, sweet, and willing to accept the leadership of the right man, but unfortunately, these men lost interest so quickly that the women in question never had a chance to reveal who they really were.

With all this in mind, I think we can agree that if you want to keep a man interested in you from the very beginning, you have to pay special attention to *what* you're communicating to the men you date. When looking for a long-term mate, men tend to rely on subtle and admittedly superficial cues to clue them in on who a woman really is at her core. A man simply will not wait around for several weeks to get to know a woman if he's already lost an attraction to her due to her dominant (masculine) behaviour on those first few dates.

If you have trouble keeping guys around longer than a few dates or weeks, you might want to consider appraising your own behaviour when interacting with men. Just like I advised in the section on 'letting your hair down', try to figure out where you might fall on the spectrum of dominant behaviours and then train yourself to seek more gracious, feminine ways to interact with men. Remember, it's not about changing who you are at your core just to get a guy. It's all about putting your best foot forward so that once his defences are lowered, he can grow to accept the real you.

When a man doesn't know you and hasn't already invested in you in some way, he'll feel less inclined to overlook something he considers a flaw or potential "red flag." When love, desire, and adoration enter the picture however, for men at least, logic gets thrown out of the window, and in the eyes of a thoroughly love-smitten man…you can do no wrong. Give love a chance to grow by accepting the way men are and not how you *wish* they were. During the first few dates, really try to see things from a man's point of view and adapt your behaviour so that you can effortlessly reveal yourself to be the kind, warm, feminine, and when the occasion calls for it, sometimes argumentative and competitive, woman of his dreams.

Reference: [2] Greenwald, Rachel. "Chapter 3/What He Said." *Have Him at Hello: Confessions from 1,000 Guys About What Makes Them Fall in Love…Or Never Call Back*, Three River Press, pp. 27–42.

Chapter 5:

When He Thinks He Can Do "Better" Than You

14

He saw you as a "backup girl."

If you've ever been in a non-relationship with a man who had the habit of weaving in and out of your life whenever he wanted, chances are you were (or are) entertaining a man who sees you as nothing more than a "backup girl." This is the guy that will pursue you with romantic gusto for a few weeks then suddenly go "dark" for a few months, without warning, only to re-emerge in a tempest of amorous attention.

Now, I'm pretty sure the moniker of "backup girl" is pretty self-explanatory, but let's define it anyway. A "backup girl" is basically a man's romantic Plan B, or C, or D, etc. She is the girl who men keep "dangling" so to speak, as she remains a man's alternative love interest when and should things go awry with the woman or wom*en* he's REALLY interested in.

In most cases, the backup girl rarely knows that she IS a backup girl. She either believes that the man she wants has "commitment issues" or he's "super busy" or he "doesn't believe in titles." Unfortunately, because she decides to entertain such fabrications, she repeatedly finds herself in dead-end relationships with unavailable men who give her just enough attention to keep her interested but who actually have no intention of ever claiming her as their girlfriend.

Why Some Women End Up as a Man's Plan 'B'

Forgive me if that definition appeared extra harsh, but this is the ugly truth. No woman who respects herself, her time, and who values her youth wants to end up as a man's "backup girl." When a woman slips into the backup girl role it could be because of any of the following reasons:

1. She lacks discretion and/or knowledge when dealing with men and how they date opportunistically.

2. She lacks strong personal boundaries when it comes to dating.

3. She has low self-esteem and is unable to recognize her true value in relationships.

4. She considers the man in question a highly desirable catch and therefore makes room for his comings and goings if it means she can have at least some of his attention.

Don't think for a moment that only licentious, uneducated, lower status, or even lesser attractive women end up as backup girls. This couldn't be further from the truth. Educated women with high-powered careers can easily find themselves as a man's Plan B if they choose to entertain such male behaviour. The same is true for the decent good girl next door and the breath-taking blonde who looks as if she could have any man she wanted. So long as a woman *chooses* to ignore the signs of becoming or being a man's backup (as such signs are blatantly obvious) her efforts to find true commitment and relationship bliss will be continually thwarted.

Signs That You Are (or May Become) a "Backup" Girl

When a woman falls into the backup girl role, she may mistakenly believe that the man she's chasing (yes, by entertaining a man who's using her, she is actually *chasing* him, albeit emotionally) is actually interested in being with her but he just can't seem to commit since he's always losing interest and withdrawing. Obviously, her confusion stems from the fact that the man in question isn't losing interest or pulling away at all. He simply has "better" dating options out there but enjoys keeping her close enough to reconnect romantically every now and then just in case his Plan A falls through.

Here are some signs that a man is trying to keep you as (or make you into) his backup girl:

1. He wants to be friends…with benefits.

2. He habitually rushes to your side and showers you with attention and heart-melting declarations of his love for you after a breakup with some other woman.

3. He believes watching Netflix at night with you, all alone with him in a dark room is him making a serious effort to woo you.

4. He's always super busy and rarely, if ever, returns your texts and phone calls.

5. He showers you with adoring compliments while admitting that you'll *"make some other guy out there happy someday."*

6. He doesn't want to be seen with you in public.

7. He reminds you about his commitment issues due to his Dad leaving/his first heartbreak/his Mom abandoning him/his friend betraying him/his pet parrot dying/etc. whenever you try to define the relationship with him.

8. He doesn't believe in titles.

9. He threatens to ignore you indefinitely and warns you that he can *"easily find a woman who'll give him what he wants"* whenever you attempt to set boundaries with him and get your needs met.

10. He doesn't hide the fact that he's dating other women.

11. He's never there when you need him...but he always expects you to be there for him.

12. He doesn't plan real dates ahead with you.

As you can see, being a man's backup girl is no place for a woman who wants to avoid a dead-end relationship and find Mr. Right while she still has her own teeth. Don't ignore the signs or be deceived. Or worse, don't rationalize a man's behaviour and so *deceive yourself.*

How to Handle a Man Who Comes and Goes as He Pleases

If you begin dating a new guy and start noticing a combination of the behaviours listed above, don't wait for him to re-emerge and thus confuse you even further. Pull the plug on this fool and don't look back. On the other hand, if you're not entirely sure that he's trying to make you a backup girl because there's just something about him that seems oh so "likable", "sweet", and "sincere" (I'm rolling my eyes, by the way), try calling him out on his behaviours. I'll be honest, **sometimes guys get into the habit of treating the women they date a certain way because they haven't yet come across a woman who had the gall to set them straight**. Men love a woman with a little moxie. Confronting a guy who wanders in and out of your life might make him recognize your high-value, which will then compel him to either leave you alone or change his ways if he wants to be with you.

So if you've got the moxie (or even if you think you don't), and you're picking up signs that Mr. Here-Today-Gone-Tomorrow is going to do one of his infamous disappearing-reappearing acts, try catching him off guard by feistily confronting him about it when he "returns" again (by the way, don't let him get away with disappearing and reappearing more than ONCE).

Whenever he tries to get in touch with you again, begin by showing him that you're not emotionally distraught or off-balanced because of his insensitive actions (disappearing and reappearing) by humorously exaggerating his ridiculous behaviour. Start off with something cheeky like this:

"Hey, it's nice to hear from you again. Haven't heard from you in months. I'm assuming you were on some sort of top-secret mission?"

Then, after he responds, make sure you bring it all home by making it clear that you won't be putting up with his insensitive actions any further.

"Listen, I like you, and I think you're a fun guy. But I'm really not a fan of being constantly led on and

abandoned like this. If you're going to disappear on me again, please know that I won't be here when you get back. I think that's fair, right?"

Boom.

Simple. Classy. Straight forward. With this response, you place him in a position where if he's really interested in you he'll have to at least agree with you and hopefully explain himself in some way. Most guys like to think themselves as being "nice" or "decent" when it comes to their interactions with women, even if their behaviour appears otherwise. Because of this, your calm but confrontational display of confidence and dignity will throw off most men and either compel them to take you seriously or simply never mess with you again (since they know that they won't be able to get away with subpar dating behaviour).

Also, keep in mind that if Mr. Here-Today-Gone-Tomorrow has any real interest in you, he'll apologize or try to explain himself while making it clear that he's still very much interested in seeing you. Standing up for yourself in this way communicates to a man that you are a high-value woman, one who values both her sanity and her dignity more than she values a man's attention. But do keep in mind that if the guy in question really doesn't see you as anything more than a backup girl, standing up for yourself will undoubtedly turn him off of you for good, which, in a situation like this...is a good thing.

15

He's taken a greater romantic interest in another woman.

When a woman comes along who a man believes is a better investment of time and energy than the one he's currently dating, he will ultimately begin pursuing her at the expense of the first woman. This is one of the more obvious reasons why men suddenly pull away and lose interest, but it is also one of the reasons men rarely ever reveal to women.

For many women, by the time they figure out that another woman was the cause for their guy's loss of interest, it's usually too late. Proof of the encroachment upon your seemingly perfect romance usually only shows up much later after Mr. McDreamy totally disappears out of your life; leaving you to slowly piece together exactly what happened. For example, after your boyfriend of one-year suddenly pulls away and calls it quits, you might start to observe him and *her* together in his Facebook pictures. You might even see him and *her* out together as if they've been in a relationship for years, or worse, a mutual friend might reveal to you that he's getting married to *her* after only four months of dating.

Listen, we've all been there at some point. You're getting to know someone and you've begun to take a real romantic interest in them only to have them suddenly pull the plug and move on to the "next best thing." It doesn't feel good, especially if you're still stuck in single and your once persistent beau is now happily dating that bombshell brunette with the perky...personality. The main thing to consider in situations like this is whether or not you were actually wronged in the first place.

Having Realistic Dating Expectations

If you've only been on a handful of dates and there hasn't been even a hint of talk about exclusivity, almost anything goes. I'm not saying this is how it should be but when you consider the prevailing self-entitled and selfish attitude of today's dating culture, this is how it is. Knowing this, so long as you're not haphazardly doling out your relationship benefits, don't allow yourself to become totally disheartened if you find out that a once persistent admirer has moved his affections to some other woman. Of course, this is always easier said than done, but if you learn to adjust your attitude to the reality of the dating culture, you're less likely to face extreme disappointments.

On the other hand, you have every right to feel hurt and enraged if you've been dating a guy consistently for several months and he bails on you for another woman without so much as a "goodbye." Sure, it might have been an awkward conversation for him to have with you, but you'd rather have some emotional closure and feel the short-term pain of rejection than suffer through the long-term pain and resentment that comes from feeling lead on and ghosted.

Unfortunately, once a guy believes he's found a woman he considers "better" and he's already pulling away from you to make space for her, there's not much you can do. The main reason it's difficult to actually take any action in such cases is because you're not going to find out he lost interest in you due to another woman until you *see* him with this new girl or hear about her through the grapevine. This is essentially the case if you've only been dating him a short while, which means he won't feel as if he owes you an explanation.

The only defence you have against such situations is to: 1. Learn how to recognize the behaviours men exhibit when they're beginning to lose interest or "fade out" of a relationship, (many which are listed in my book, *He's Not That Interested, He's Just Passing Time*) and... 2. Once you *do* find out that he's slowly creating an exit from the relationship you must cease to entertain him and take your precious time and affections elsewhere.

When Courtship Lacks Courtesy

For a woman, the most hurtful thing about this sort of situation is that guys do not always *end* a previous relationship until the affections of the new woman have been clearly established. This is the reason why you may feel as if there is still a chance to make things work with a man, even if he's beginning to show signs of a loss of interest in you. Once they've come across a woman they feel is better suited for them, being opportunistic by nature, most guys won't find it *in their best interest* to inform the woman they're presently dating that she's merely a placeholder until they can fully secure the affections and desire of the new girl.

A gentleman on the other hand, once he realizes there's another woman he'd like to date would, in fact, realize that he doesn't see you as an ideal mate, and would therefore stop seeing you as soon as possible so as to not waste any more of your time. The mature gentleman would make this clear to you as soon as he could, breaking the news to you graciously in hopes of sparing you the pain of ambiguity. Therefore, if a man is sincere and honest enough to politely inform you that, *"I know we're having fun, and while you do mean a lot to me, I still think we're better suited for other people"*, consider yourself lucky, as most women don't experience this sort of candour in today's confrontation-avoidant dating culture.

Chapter 6:

How to Understand Men and the Way They Date

Men Don't "Fall in Love" the Way Women Do

Contrary to popular belief, men tend to experience the romantic feelings of "falling in love" before women do. We also tend to experience romantic attraction far more intensely as well, at least during the early stages. As a woman, these distinctions are vitally important to know because being familiar with what a man *feels* during the early stages of a blossoming romance will help you to think and act more clearly in the midst of his overpowering and highly persuasive romantic intensity.

A very insightful article on PsychologyToday.com [3] points to a research study that sheds some light on the true nature of men's romantic feelings vs women's. The study was published in the *Journal of Social Psychology*, where researchers, Marissa A. Harrison and Jennifer C. Shortall, studied men and women in love and asked a series of questions regarding the love dynamics of romantic relationships. When the question was asked: *"In your most recent romantic relationship, how long did it take you to realize you were in love?"* the results showed that men stated that they fell in love far more quickly than women.

Another question was asked of the subjects, which was: *"In your most recent committed, romantic relationship, who said 'I love you' FIRST?"* The results showed that more men (64%) had admitted to saying 'I love you' first than did the women (19%), while only 12% of the subjects admitted that neither them nor their partners had said these words at all.

This study helps to shed at least some light on men's "coming on strong" behavior, as many women tend to believe guys are being disingenuous when they do come on strong only to suddenly lose interest and disappear without a trace. I think this is a common misconception among women who experience the disappearing acts of men. Sure, some guys only come on strong to convince you of their devotion, get something from you, and move on, but chances are that the majority of guys you date are going to "come on strong" simply because of their primal programming when it comes to finding a mate.

For men, romantic love usually starts early and continues onward throughout a relationship. Men don't "fall in love" gradually, as popular culture tends to promote. Sure, we take a while to become emotionally attached to a woman and to become thoroughly convinced of her long-term value to us. But when it comes to pure **romantic attraction**, it is pretty much love at first sight, or in most cases, love after a handful of fun, casual dates.

Also, keep in mind that I'm not talking about pure lust here. That's the kind of thing where a man sees a woman and is overwhelmed with a strong desire to simply have sex with her. No. I'm talking about romantic attraction, where a man desires a woman physically but he also craves her emotional closeness, her company, and maybe even has hopes of making her his long-term companion.

While a man may ask you out solely based on his physical attraction to you, within a surprisingly limited number of dates he can assess whether or not he desires greater intimacy, closeness, and long-term companionship with you. When he first lays eyes on you, he's subconsciously determining if you're his "type" and if his attraction to you is worth the risk of possible

111

rejection. But once you decide to go out with him a few times, on each of these occasions his romantic attraction to you is based on your personal and interpersonal energy, or, put another way – *how you make him feel*.

Men need to be wired this way because it benefits our particular biological needs in successfully passing on our genes. In order for our genes to survive and flourish, we need to be able to assess a woman's mating and nurturing potential in as little time possible. Thus, our primal attraction to a woman is based on how we perceive her factors of fertility (ability to reproduce), the factors that make her a capable mate and mother (ability to nurture), and the factors that make her a trustworthy carrier of our progeny and ours alone (ability to remain monogamous). Thus, the faster a man can assess these factors the greater success he'll have at passing his genes along to the next generation.

Women on the other hand tend to experience the romantic feelings of falling in love much more slowly. This is both natural and necessary because her **primal mating drives** are based on her desire to secure the love and loyalty of a strong and capable man, one who has the highest potential to offer her security (physical, material, sexual, emotional, etc.) in the world. To successfully secure such a man, she must observe and test him over an extended period of time. Thus, for her to experience the same depth of feelings of romantic attraction, she needs to see first-hand, a consistent display of a man's strength, confidence, intelligence, love, devotion, and even his dominance over other men in order to feel safe with and supportive of him.

I know this all doesn't sound very sexy, but when you realize that your dream guy's romantic behavior is being driven by his primal programming it's a lot easier to remind yourself that even though it appears as if he's in love with you, it's nothing more than him being drugged up on a hormonal concoction of primal love emotions. These very same emotions will continue to fog his better judgment concerning you as he tries to determine whether or not he's really *ready* to commit.

Knowing that a man might experience the feelings of falling in love much faster, you can avoid getting easily swept up by his romantic intensity, thus allowing you to respond to his emotionally-driven advances in a more tactical and advantageous fashion.

Believe me, he wants you to playfully fend him off just enough to keep him engaged but unsatisfied. I know it sounds like a "game", but it really isn't. You're simply adjusting your dating strategy to appeal not only to his primal programming, but his *better nature*. If you take his romantic intensity at face value and quickly give up your friends, hobbies, career, commitments, and relationship benefits (whatever they are) for him, he WILL feel satisfied, but also…disappointed. I'm convinced that most guys have no idea that they're wired this way, which is why men sometimes feel disappointed and even remorseful after the woman they've been chasing falls for them prematurely.

By being *resistant* or even unwilling to give up certain aspects of your life for him and by being *slow* to offer him your relationship benefits, so long as he's serious about you, you can actually fuel his romantic attraction and make him even more determined to make you his and his alone. Believe me, you have more power than you can imagine when it comes to attracting and keeping the guy you want.

Therefore, no matter how dreamy you think he is and how you so don't want to risk losing him by *not* giving him what he wants, don't ruin a blossoming romance by allowing a guy to get exactly what he wants from you **when he wants it**. When his commitment feels right to you, feel free to give him your heart so long as you do so on your terms (which is why it is important for a woman to know exactly what her terms are). If he truly respects and wants you, he'll only want you more when you make him work to win your heart (and everything else).

Now, I know it can be hard sometimes to stick to your principles when your heart (and everything else) seems to burn with passion for a particular guy. But I implore you, DO NOT make excuses for a man just because of his handsomeness, status, wealth, race, background, promises, sexual chemistry, etc. Relationship-minded men are attracted to women with principles, the kind of women who could care less about how much money a man makes or how devilishly charming and sought-after he is.

Don't make excuses for a guy who seems impatient with you, no matter how fearful you are of losing him. The men who will love you unconditionally are the ones who will respect your principles and your boundaries. A man's apparent impatience is sometimes a test to see what kind of woman you are. So don't let his frustration instil you with fear. If he cannot accept your rules of engagement, **he doesn't want a relationship with you that badly**. Remember that.

Men are the Gatekeepers of Commitment

According to Dr. David D. Gilmore's book, *Manhood in the Making: Cultural Concepts of*

Masculinity, one of the three pillars of manhood is 'to procreate' (the others being 'to protect' and 'to provide' in case you were curious). Consequently, in order to procreate, men need and will perpetually pursue sex. And in order to get the sex he requires, a man must be willing to endure the trials and tribulations that come with trying to attract, seduce, and "procreate" with the woman of his choice. Why is it that men throughout history have viewed this mating ritual as an important task that requires effort, skill, and mastery? Simple. It's because women have been, and always will be, the gatekeepers of sexual pleasure.

This is why men are considered the "pursuers" when it comes to romantic relationships, and it is also the reason why men read more books about "how to attract women" and "how to seduce women" rather than books about "how to build a relationship" with women. Men know that it's WAY more difficult to spark intense romantic interest in a high-value woman than it is to make her desire a commitment once a mutual attraction has been established.

In fact, if we're all being honest here, generally, once a woman is deeply romantically interested in a man, she will begin to harbor fantasies of what a future relationship with him might look like. Men on the other hand, usually don't share this sentiment. Sure, we might feel the *feelings* of being in love first and foremost, but these emotions are a function of our primal programming (the need to mate with a low-risk-high-reward female) and thus we tend to live in the moment more often than women do.

The thing is, men face MORE rejection during the preliminary stages of the dating game because they are tasked with the challenge of approaching a woman they find attractive and sparking sexual desire within her. Because women are the gatekeepers of sex and the male mating strategy forces us to prioritize physical attraction first and foremost, we face greater levels of rejection, failure, loss, and frustration than a woman ever will **during the initial phases of courtship**.

Women on the other hand, face MORE rejection once mutual romantic interest has been established in some capacity. This is because men are the gatekeepers of commitment. And since a woman's mating strategies force her to prioritize sexual and material security through a man's commitment; she faces greater levels of rejection, failure, loss, and frustration than a man ever will once a mutual romantic interest has been established.

If you can accept this premise, you can better empathize with what men go through in dating and relationships. We face rejection in the beginning of a potential courtship, usually at point blank range, as it is embedded deep within human culture for a man to be proactive in securing the amorous affections and devotion of a willing female. Women face greater rejection once those "amorous affections" have been mutually established, however, as the very man that was so proactive about stealing your heart could end up leaving it right where he found it.

This all may sound harsh, and it might be a difficult pill to swallow, but accepting that this is how things are will allow you to set better boundaries with men. By accepting that this is simply the way of men, you will have far more realistic expectations whenever a guy takes an interest in you, begins to fall for you, and starts

116

to sell you a dream. Don't let a man sell you a dream.

Remember, a man who begins pursuing you should be categorized as being 'typical' until he proves himself otherwise. So unless he begs you for exclusivity and invests both emotional and physical equity into the relationship, then he must remain categorically, 'typical', and therefore…not a major factor in your life.

Men Will Take the Path of Least Resistance

As you can expect from human nature, men, just like women, will take the path of least resistance more often than not. What this means is that a man is less likely to inform you when he has lost interest, and instead he'll probably resort to ghosting you entirely. Granted, this won't always be the case with every man you come across, but if you at least *assume* that the men you meet might act in this way, you're less likely to experience the hurt, anger, and frustrating disappointment that comes after a man disappears on you.

Some men live their lives to avoid as much conflict and confrontation as humanly possible. They'd rather completely dissolve a relationship in silence than confront a woman with the uncomfortable truth. "Nice Guys" tend to fall into this category especially because they'd rather not look like the "bad guy" in any kind of dating scenario. They believe that they can somehow make a woman believe they're a "good person" by simply ghosting on her instead of actually being honest and upfront. They believe that going silent on a woman is always the best option. Since by doing so they believe they can avoid hurting your feelings *directly*, avoid an uncomfortable conversation/argument, and walk away with the belief that they "let you down easy", which in their minds makes them a "pretty nice guy."

Men are More Comfortable with Casual

In general, men are a lot more comfortable with casual relationships than are most women. A man can be quite content dating a woman for an insane amount of time, knowing full well that she's not, "The One." Unless the woman in question puts up a fuss, he'd rarely, if ever, stop and wonder if he was leading her on or wasting her time. In reality, unless a man has reached that point in his life where he's **proactively** searching for Mrs. Right, most men really don't lose sleep wondering if the woman they're dating is, "The One."

The average man also doesn't lose sleep pondering concepts like "wasted youth" or "biological clock". Concepts such as these are so foreign to most guys that they rarely stop to consider if their interest in you might actually jeopardize your future happiness. And because this isn't something men are familiar with, let alone fearful of, they simply cannot relate to women and therefore possess very little capacity to actually care.

I say this to point out the fact that you cannot assume that men understand what a woman goes through when she's been led on for an extended amount of time only to be dumped or ghosted unceremoniously. The average man won't have this particular aspect of your best interest in mind not because he's a selfish idiot, but because he's simply oblivious and uninformed to the things that women deal with when dating. Naturally, because he's completely oblivious to a woman's deepest primal fears when it comes to finding a mate, he won't feel any pressure or responsibility to date her in a way that would at least allow her to preserve her dignity should things not work out.

Also, for truly opportunistic men, they won't have any qualms telling you exactly what you want to hear in order to keep you interested in them. But why would they go through all the trouble to keep you interested if they don't want you for a lifetime? Simple. They want you close enough to reap the benefits of being with you (whatever those benefits might be), while ensuring that can keep their options open as well. This is why it's so important for a woman to carefully observe the things a man does rather than focus on what he says. Doing so will help you to avoid succumbing to the sweet, seductive, and even sincere things a man might say, even though he's ultimately incapable of giving you the kind of commitment you truly desire.

Reference: [3] Saad, Gad. "Who Utters 'I Love You' First: Men or Women?" Web article. *PsychologyToday*. December 27 2011. Web. January 2019.

Chapter 7:

How to Avoid the Pitfalls of Romantic Love

Don't Rely on Chemistry Alone

Many women fall for a man based **solely** on the way he makes her *feel*. This is especially true for those who have difficulty filtering for Mr. Right and judging a man's true intentions. Often their inexperience with choosing the right man causes these women to rely on the amount of chemistry they feel with a guy as the most important factor in determining his relationship worth. Unfortunately, relying on chemistry alone is NOT an effective method for determining a man's relationship potential or his reliability as a romantic partner.

As wonderful as it may seem to be with a man who can make you *feel* a plethora of beautiful, passionate, and euphoric emotions, those very same emotions are often *extremely* misleading when determining a man's true worth to you. If you get so caught up in how a man makes you feel on the inside, you may fail to properly assess how things really look on the outside when it comes to the nature of the relationship (assuming one even exists). The chemistry we feel for someone is ephemeral in nature, and thus, an unreliable marker of future relationship happiness.

For example, through his in-depth studies and research, author and relationship psychologist, Ty Tashiro, explored the key factors individuals should look for when choosing an ideal mate. In his book, *The Science of Happily Ever After: What Really Matters in the Quest for Enduring Love*, Tashiro concludes that a strong focus on compatibility as opposed to chemistry is what truly determines both the happiness and the longevity of romantic relationships. In his research, he makes a clear distinction between "lust" (which chemistry helps to create) verses "liking" (which stems from compatibility), and how a focus on the latter leads to greater **long-term success** in love and romance.

While this all may *seem* like common sense at first glance, let's get really honest for a moment. How often do you (or your girlfriends) pursue relationships with men that drive you crazy in a good way, even though they also drive you crazy in a bad way? You might be thinking that it's quite natural to have the "bad crazy" come with the "good crazy", but don't be misled.

There's a big difference between the solvable relationship conflicts that arise from couple disputes than the more serious "bad crazy" conflicts that stem from serious incompatibility issues and interpersonal dysfunction. While chemistry will get you in the door and grease the gears of romance to help love blossom, it's really the strength of your compatibility with a particular man that will determine the stability and potential longevity of a relationship.

By the way, if it seems as if I'm beating up on "the women" and being a bit one-sided, believe me, I'm not. Men also fall prey to how a particular woman might make them feel and thus fail to see the obvious red flags that might make her extremely incompatible or even detrimental to his future happiness. The difference for men however, is that it's easier for them to continue seeing a woman in-spite of the knowledge that she might be incompatible and thus, not "The One."

As I already mentioned in the previous section, most men aren't concerned about "wasted time", "biological clocks", or "feeling used" as do women. Because of this, assuming sex is in the equation, they may still choose to continue seeing a woman who they've already determined is NOT the kind of woman they can or ever will, commit to.

I only mention this to show you that, yes, while a man might get deeply involved with a woman based mostly on the chemistry he feels with her, the stakes are potentially much lower for him than it will be for the woman involved. Getting yourself hooked on a guy because of the killer chemistry you're feeling with him is great, but always keep in mind that chemistry wanes easily over time – the very same 'time' that you can never get back.

Be Wary of a Man's Romantic Intensity

Once you understand and come to terms with the fact that a man's primary interest in you will be first and foremost 'sexual' in nature, you will have a much easier time seeing through his overwhelmingly convincing (though often misleading) romantic intensity at the beginning of a new love affair. When a man first takes an obvious interest in you, he is being driven by his desire for sexual conquest. I use the term "conquest" because this is **how men think**. If a man is giving off clear signs that he's romantically interested in you, his "chasing" you is merely the product of his primal urge to procreate with you and claim you sexually. I'm not saying that this is the ONLY thing a man might be after, but you must strongly assume and accept that this is both the PRIMARY and the DOMINANT emotion that is dictating his behaviour towards you.

Generally, for men, the desire for sexual conquest is just as strong (if not stronger) as the desire women have for relationship security. Also keep in mind that the things that make a woman a strong candidate for sexual conquest are much simpler (and therefore faster to evaluate for a man) than those things that make her a strong candidate for a serious commitment. Thus, when a man is "coming on strong" he's simply being compelled by sexual attraction. The mistake many women often make is that they translate a man's 'coming on strong' as *"he wants to be with me and only me"* when, based on the nature of men, is not necessarily the case.

If you translate a man's romantic intensity as a clear sign that he's ready for a serious commitment, don't be surprised when he eventually disappears soon after you give in to his passions. The amorous powers and purposes that are drawing him toward you, at least at the beginning of a love affair, are not the same as the ones that are drawing you toward him. So don't wishfully believe that his romantic intensity is a clear sign that he wants what YOU want.

In the beginning stages of a new romance, a man hasn't been around you long enough to establish your true value as a compatible, long-term partner. More importantly, neither has he had enough time to become deeply *emotionally attached* to you. Both of these things are *necessary* requirements for a man to truly fall in love with a woman AND commit to being with her above all other women. This is why succumbing to a man's seductions before both his heart and mind have been unified and subdued by your unique brand of female love and tenderness will result in his loss of interest in you.

It benefits a woman immensely to know these things because it allows her to think more clearly and therefore act more judiciously with the men that take an interest in her. Without adopting the notion that a man's romantic intensity is merely the product of his desire to procreate, a woman often remains at the mercy of her emotions. Because of a man's romantic intensity, she may be persuaded to believe that, *"because he calls and texts me, takes me out to dinner and pays, flirts with me daily, shares his dreams with me, holds my hand in public, and prioritizes me over his friends...**he must want a relationship with me**."*

And yes, while such actions could come from a man who wants a *serious* relationship with you, **do not assume that a man who only wanted sex couldn't possibly act this way as well**. It is this belief that causes women to give their all to men *prematurely* as they become addicted to guys who exhibit unrelenting romantic intensity. It's a bitter pill to swallow, but you must understand that men aren't necessarily evil or determined to use you and waste your time. They are simply being driven by a primal urge, one that masks its self-serving nature in the form of insistent romantic desire. The kind of romantic desire that, unfortunately for many women, is often misread and therefore misunderstood.

Don't Be Timid When Setting Your Standards

While I believe that a woman should strive to be flexible, congenial, and generally easy-to-please to ensure that a man finds her extremely likable and therefore, "relationship material", I also believe she should also strive to be both confident and consistent when it comes to enforcing her personal boundaries. While "niceness" is an extremely important quality of female behaviour men look for *very* early in a new romance, they will also secretly test a woman to determine her standards. High-quality men want an easy-going woman, but not a doormat.

These men want a woman with whom they can easily get along with, but who can also confidently tell them (or others) "NO" when she needs to. They want a woman who can communicate her relationship needs clearly and who can also express her dissatisfactions graciously. High-quality men desire the kind of woman who can maintain her poise and magnanimity even amidst the hostility of others; one who can resolutely resist a man when his amorous advances threaten her dignity, or dismiss him entirely if he repeatedly treats her with disdain and disrespect.

Trust me, great guys LOVE IT when a woman has high but reasonable standards. This is because it communicates that she's **genuinely** "hard-to-get" and thus, must be worth the extra effort required to woo her. This is why you shouldn't be fearful about scaring away most men with your particular brand of boundaries.

Does it really matter if you scare away "most" men? You're not interested in "most" men; you're interested in attracting the man who finds you irresistible and who is willing to do whatever it takes to keep you in his life. If your boundaries are **reasonable** and **important** to you, so long as you communicate them with clarity, confidence, courteousness, and consistency, the right guy will find your brand of standards both beautiful and worth the effort.

For example, if you don't deep kiss guys who aren't your boyfriend, whenever a not-yet-boyfriend makes a go at your lips, ensure that you turn your cheek to him and flirtatiously inform him about this dating standard of yours. Another example: if you "don't send nudes", graciously let him know this fact if a guy attempts to get one from you during a texting conversation. These are just very simple examples to be sure, but any sort of dating boundary such as these needs to be clearly communicated and enforced consistently, as this is the key to communicating your high self-respect and true worth to a man when he first begins to take a romantic interest in you.

You see, at the beginning of a new romance, a guy knows very little about you, but he's both deeply curious and immensely determined to get what he wants. The more allowances you make for him, granting him free passes because of his status, wealth, ethnicity, handsomeness, etc., the less he'll believe what you tell him, at least when it comes to what you will or will not stand for.

Another example: if you said you'd meet a guy at a particular place at such and such a time and he doesn't show up at a reasonable time, ensure that you don't waste your day/night waiting for him to show up. Leave within a thirty to forty-minute buffer (depending on the venue) and wait for him to contact you. If he's really interested he will offer up a **valid excuse**, apologize, and ask you out again (and I guarantee you he won't be late again). If he's not really that interested he won't follow up, as he will probably hold the self-entitled belief that you should have waited on him indefinitely. In other words, you'll leave him with the impression that you're, *"way too much work."*

Listen, don't worry if some men, especially in the earlier stages, see you as *"too much work."* This is a good thing. I believe women should have a cutthroat approach when it comes to filtering low-interest/romantically-lazy men as quickly as possible. By doing so you can avoid wasting your time, as making allowances for low-interest and ambivalent men will give them the room they need to slowly breakdown your emotional barriers and work their way into your heart and more.

Chapter 8:

How to Protect Your Dignity

and Win with Men

Let Him Chase You for a Relationship

If you have just begun seeing a guy and he appears to be pursuing you quite passionately, your only job is to remain "neutral" with him *until* the "sale" has been made (the "sale" being where he asks for an exclusive relationship). Being "neutral" means you're not getting caught up in his "salesmanship" of emotions and desire. Instead, you remain visibly content with your singleness by not giving up your friends, hobbies, commitments, and in some cases...the other guy you might be casually dating as well.

Don't let your behaviours reveal just how really infatuated you are with him just yet. Fight and subdue your natural instincts to reciprocate his displays of passion **and stay neutral about his intentions until your new guy asks (or begs) you to be his girlfriend**. Only after Mr. McDreamy has become so emotionally invested in you that he cannot stand the thought of some other guy stealing your heart away will he desire exclusivity.

Now, when I say stay "neutral", I don't mean to become a zombie and not show him any signs of your interest in him at all. Being neutral simply means that you're giving him the opportunity to figure out if he really wants to be with you or not. You probably missed that, so let me repeat it: Being neutral simply means that you are giving him the opportunity to figure out if he really wants to be with you or not. What this means is that:

1. You are very receptive of his texts and phone calls so long as they're not interfering with your work, school, present engagements, personal

hobbies, etc.

2. You are very receptive of his attempts to spend time with you so long as he is not interfering with your work, school, friendships, family, present engagements, etc.

3. You are very receptive of his flirting and romantic advances so long as they don't threaten your dignity or cross a personal boundary (such as no French-kissing guys who aren't boyfriends, no texting nude photos, etc.).

4. And you are very receptive of his desire to emotionally and physically protect and provide for you in thoughtful and endearing ways so long as, again, his actions do not threaten your dignity or cross a personal boundary of yours.

As you can see, being neutral until a guy begs to be your boyfriend simply means that you should first be receptive (not proactive) **then willing to reciprocate** whenever your new Mr. McDreamy does something to illustrate his sincere romantic interest in you. Don't just be receptive, but show him just how happy he makes you and how appreciative you are of his interest by reciprocating only after he's made a move towards you. **Let him lead**.

Now, if a guy you've just begun dating is a lot less enthusiastic, meaning he's "playing it cool" or even acting somewhat aloof or half-hearted in his attempts to win your heart, instead of being "neutral" what you actually want to do is become a little more "negative" by swinging even further away from him. You do this by ensuring that his attempts to secure your attention are not even remotely half-hearted. If you have already gone out on at least one or two dates and you want to know if Mr. McDreamy "like likes" you, pay close attention to see if he's enthusiastic to spend more time with you, not just privately, but publicly as well.

For example, a guy who wants to play it cool will try to make plans with you at the last minute. This is the guy who will text you (why isn't he *calling* you, by the way?) with plans to meet up that night or some other time when you least expect it. At first you might think that this sort of spontaneous behaviour is actually kind of romantic, but that's part of the reason why some men do it.

Experienced men know that creating romantic scenarios for women as well as placing them in romantic situations is the key to success when it comes to seduction. But remember, you're not trying to be *seduced* just yet. You're trying to be *convinced* of his true intentions. Placing you in romantic situations adds fuel to your female infatuation, which may cause you to compromise your better judgment regarding Mr. Play-It-Cool.

So instead of allowing this behaviour, you simply swing "negative" and rebuff his last-minute requests to see you. You can simply inform him that you have other plans or that it's too last minute. Or you can sweet-it-up by telling him something like, *"Nate, I like hanging out with you. I think you're fun, but I'll have to pass. It's difficult for me to see you at the last minute. I want to see more of you, but I need you to give me a bit more heads up in the future. I think that's fair, right?"* Boom. Simple, sweet, sincere, and most importantly…it shows him that you have standards.

If a man is genuinely interested in you, telling him something like this will cause both his respect for and attraction to you to SKYROCKET immediately. Men know that only a woman with options, a great single life, and high self-esteem can brazenly insist that she be treated in a more thoughtful way. Of course, if Mr. Play-It-Cool was not that interested in you, he might think you are "too much work" and decide to move on to more easy prey, but I guarantee you that he will at least walk away with a deep respect for you.

Now, I do understand that there might be instances where a guy just found out about some cool, time-sensitive activity and he wants you to come with him to check it out, but instances like these are the exceptions. Thus, if you get the impression that this is a guy's default method of making plans with you, resist the urge to make constant allowances for him, no matter how tall, dark, and handsome you think he is.

Also, keep in mind that a man may be genuinely and deeply interested in you but might be a bit more experienced with women to know that it's in his best interest to "play things cool." While this is a great seduction technique to use for the nice guy who truly does want you, keep in mind that players, time wasters, and ambivalent men also use it as well to their advantage. Because you will have no reliable way to tell whether or not Mr. Play-It-Cool is a nice guy who *really* wants you or if he's a player or time waster, swinging against him and staying "negative" is the most effective weapon in your seduction arsenal to filter a man's true intentions.

How to Handle the "Slow Decline" of an Eventual Break Up

There may come a time where you have been dating a guy for quite a while, perhaps nine months or more, and he suddenly begins to pull away from you. While handling a situation like this is a bit more stressful and nerve-wracking because of all the time, love, and energy you've already invested in him and the relationship, it should still be handled with the same amount of tact and cleverness as would have been required if you two were just dating casually.

Let's say that over several weeks, you notice that your boyfriend calls you less and less and doesn't make time to see you as much as he used to. Or worse, let's say that his behaviour has become more standoffish and inconsiderate as of late, where he does things like leave town with his buddies without so much as a polite heads-up to let you know about it.

You want to address such declining interest *immediately* and courageously so that he doesn't grow to believe that you are accepting of such treatment. At this point, all you need to do is simply have a heart-to-heart talk with your boyfriend and ask him what's going on. You want to give him the benefit of the doubt first and foremost because he might have had a stressful change happen in his life that's causing him to neglect the relationship.

But let's say you've called him, and after having had a sincere talk with him to figure out what's going on you've come to the conclusion that he isn't really stressed about anything other than the fact that he's not as sold on you as he once was, or, in other words, he wants to break up with you. What you want to do at this point is ensure that you deal with the situation with the utmost poise and grace and force him to dismiss you in a dignified manner.

Let me explain.

You see, you have to expect the man you're dating to act like a man, even if he's breaking up with you. You should expect to be treated honourably simply because you respect both him and yourself far too much to allow him to dismiss you in an undignified fashion. The thing is, if you've been dating a guy exclusively for any length of time, especially over six months, unless you cheated on the poor guy there's absolutely no reason he should break up with you over the phone, or worse, via text.

For example, if he texts you some sad message about "seeing other people" or attempts to break up with you by phone, stop him mid-sentence and insist that he discuss it with you in person. Assuming your relationship was actually halfway decent, there is no reason for him to take the coward's way out and brush you under the rug like a clump of dirt. So again, expect him to behave in a manner fitting of a mature adult male and *insist* that he have "the talk" with you in person. A woman of your calibre deserves at least that much. You can accept a man's rejection, but never accept disrespectful treatment.

When you do meet with him, take the highroad. Be civil, be reasonable, and maintain a dignified disposition. You don't have to pretend as if you aren't hurt or saddened to see him go, but never stoop to begging, whining, or using tears as a way to guilt-trip him into staying. Just hold onto your emotions and handle the situation as best as you can, preferably like a mature adult female.

Finally, and most importantly, once the break-up is over, your once-boyfriend must now **cease to exist**. I cannot stress this enough. In fact, if this were an elementary classroom I'd make you write this sentence one-hundred times on a chalkboard: *No matter how happy, sad, nostalgic, angry, or indifferent I feel and no matter how rational my reasons may appear for doing so…under NO circumstance will I ever contact my ex-boyfriend.* The only thing contacting a man who has already rejected you does is make him more confident with his decision to leave you and more indifferent towards you, as your reaching out to him will undoubtedly reaffirm what he already believes about you: that he can do better than you.

The thing is, by not contacting him you *may* have a chance at getting him back. Assuming your relationship with him was actually good, he will always have a hint of doubt in the back of his mind as he wonders if he really did leave the woman that was actually perfect for him. Not chasing him and getting on with your life is the surest way to test his true devotion.

Without any confirmations that he made a good decision (since you've decided to cut him off), he will have to conclude that you truly were a high-quality woman, one who values her dignity far more than she does the desire of any particular man. And once he realizes he could never do better than you and that he truly did cherish what he once shared with you, he will eventually run back to you with the intention of never letting go again.

Now you might be wondering why you should even go through the trouble of getting a guy to break up with you in a dignified fashion. You may even be thinking, *"Well, if he doesn't want me, to hell with him! Good riddance."* Of course, you'd be justified in your feelings, but not allowing a man to pull away and eventually break up with you in such a thoughtless way actually works in your favour.

The benefit of confronting him is that it makes him see you as being *different* from other women, different in a very good way. If he attempts to dump you through text, email, or the phone, I can guarantee you that he's probably done it to other women in the past. There's a high chance that none of those women ever confronted him about it or worse, if they did confront him they might have become hysterical or desperate.

Years of personal experience, social observations, research, and listening to women discuss their issues regarding men has revealed one very important thing that I honestly believe most women overlook when dealing with the opposite sex, and it's this: **Men will treat you exactly the way you allow them to. Every. Single. Time. And once they realize they can get away with subpar behaviour, *you*, as a romantic partner, become subpar to them.** Put another way, in the mind of a man, a woman's value as a long-term romantic partner is directly related to the quality of behaviours she expects and accepts from her romantic partner. Let that sink in.

I mention this to show you why it's so important to insist on being treated with respect from a man, even in a situation like this. If you allow him to break up with you in an undignified fashion, your value will continue to drop in his eyes, and thus, you will lose a potential opportunity to pull him back. Forcing him to break things off in a dignified fashion will not only communicate to him just how highly you think of yourself, but how highly you think of him as well. And if there's one thing ALL high-quality men desire, it's to be with a woman who, because of her own high self-worth, can bring out the best in us, even if she has no way of possibly benefitting from it.

Final Thoughts:

A Tale of Two Love-Worthy

Women

The Right Mental Attitude for Winning with Men

Men sometimes pull away from relationships and lose interest in the women they date. It happens. And although women tend to do it to men as well, it's something that women are more likely to struggle with due to the fact that men are the gatekeepers of commitment. This is the reality, and a more sobering reality is that men will never truly understand how much it hurts you when they lead you on (whether intentionally or unintentionally) only to dismiss you unceremoniously or disappear without a trace.

But even though this is the reality, as a woman, you still possess an immense amount of power when a man begins pulling away from you. And this power comes from one very simple thing: **the meaning you give to the situation.**

The meaning you give to a man pulling away will determine how well you handle the situation. It doesn't matter if he's just begun to lose interest or if he's already disappeared off the face of the earth. The meaning you give to these scenarios will determine just how successful you are at pulling a man back to you or recovering from a dead investment.

No guy you've been dating for just four weeks should be able to completely obliterate your self-esteem by going ghost on you (especially if you didn't have sex with him). You may feel disrespected and even a bit miffed, but once you don't attach a negative meaning to the situation, your self-esteem should remain intact even after your short love affair with him has ended. Of course, if your boyfriend of two intense years begins pulling away from you, that's another story. But even in the face of an impending break-up with a long-term beau, placing a negative meaning on the situation will render you powerless when you attempt to pull him back or recover from losing him.

The meaning we give situations in life are determined by what we subconsciously believe about the world around us and ourselves. These beliefs are the product of our past experiences, our present values, our insecurities, and the ideas we adopt from others.

Every time a man pulls away or disappears, you have a choice. You have to imagine it as a fork in the road, where one bright path leads you to a positive meaning of the situation and the other path takes you down a rabbit hole of negativity. The path you choose will determine how you respond to the situation and thus, your capacity to handle it judiciously.

The Dating Adventures of Sophia & Judy

Let's observe a young lady named Sophia. Sophia's been dating a guy for six months exclusively, and all of a sudden, he begins hanging out with his guy friends more and her less. He's only pulling away emotionally because he pursued her so ardently over the first few months that he neglected his friends, but has recently been feeling the need to reconnect with them and replenish his masculine energies.

If Sophia instantly attaches a negative meaning to the situation, her first response will be to *do more* to get more of his time and attention. Her boyfriend is already feeling stifled because he's been spending so much time with her, but Sophia begins to exacerbate the problem by calling him more, sending him more romantic texts, showing up to his "guy time" functions unannounced with treats and goodies, placing pictures of them together in his apartment, and other *seemingly* sweet and endearing behaviors.

When this doesn't work, she attaches more negative meaning to the situation and begins to grow sullen, anxious, and irritated at him because he's not reciprocating her love. Even though she tries to hide it, she becomes visibly agitated and testy whenever he attempts to spend time with his friends, put in more time at work, or makes any other plans that don't directly involve her. She begins to question his love for her, and as her worry grows her attitude changes from calm to fretful and from loving to possessive.

Her boyfriend doesn't know what's bubbling *beneath* her surface, but *on* the surface, to him it seems as if his once sweet and loving girlfriend has become controlling and unreasonable, which ultimately causes him to lose some of his attraction to her. Feeling even more stifled than before, his attempts to reason with her ultimately fail, as Sophia's negativity sabotages her ability to communicate with him. Due to their on-going lack of understanding, a break-up is inevitable, even though deep down neither really wants to call it quits.

But let's look at Judy who, because of her high self-esteem, dating experience, and deep understanding of men, has developed the habit of attaching positive meanings to her experiences with men and dating. Now Judy admits that she's had a string of dead investment romances with three guys over the past several months. All of them appeared seriously interested in her at first, and then suddenly lost interest at some point. For Judy, however, each experience either taught her something about herself or about the men in general.

For example, the first guy was a complete waste of time. She went on three dates with him whereby after the third date she never heard back from the guy. She texted him a few times, but received nothing back except radio silence. She eventually figured that his loss of interest probably had something to do with the fact that she turned down his flattering yet presumptuous invitation to spend the night at his apartment after date number three. She shrugs it off, knowing that she dodged a bullet with that one.

The second guy helped her realize that she can come on a bit too strong, as he tried to disappear on her after she began to initiate most of the phone calls and even showed up at his work with homemade food for impromptu romantic lunches. She was disappointed when he lost interest, but contacted him to learn the truth. Her insistence on getting the truth from him (and to not be dismissed in such an undignified fashion) helped her to look at her behavior more objectively.

The third guy stayed around for two months longer and was really into her. For reasons unknown to her, however, he started to pull away once they become exclusive, but Judy backed off and did not chase him in any way. He came back, but then two months later he started to pull away again and even went a full week without contacting her. At this point, Judy put her foot down and calmly insisted that they should see other people, as she was more interested in a relationship with a mature adult male rather than an emotional rollercoaster.

Although Judy did miss him several weeks later because of their phenomenal chemistry, she knew better than to contact an ex and decided it was best to move on both physically and emotionally. She admittedly wondered if something was wrong with her since she kept losing seemingly great guys, but after a day or two of introspection she came to two powerful conclusions that:

- If a guy was not clear that he wanted her as enthusiastically as she wanted him...she wouldn't waste her time, and...

- She would not chase a man by rewarding his ambivalent behavior with *more* attention, *more* love, and *more* favors, etc.

Reaching these empowering conclusions, she decided that it was better to be contentedly single than to be somebody's 'passing time' girl, consolation prize, or even their beautiful distraction. After making this mental shift, Judy spent the next few months accepting as many dates with men as she could. **She kept an open-mind but remained true to her high but reasonable standards, regardless of the chemistry or apparent quality of the guy she was seeing.** She stuck to her guns and quickly dismissed dissipated, ambivalent, and romantically lazy men while making herself *slowly* more available to guys who treated her (and others) with consummate respect and kindness.

Following this dating regimen, Judy eventually started dating Simon. He pursued her passionately, respected her clearly communicated and enforced boundaries, and offered her an exclusive relationship after one and a half months of going out with her on *real* dates.

Simon didn't lose interest once he became a boyfriend, but as is the nature of life, his work, commitments, and other relationships would sometimes pull his focus too far away from Judy and their relationship. Whenever this happened, Judy held her poise and refrained from attaching negative meanings to the lulls in their relationship. She simply gave him the space he needed to miss her which would draw Simon back to her naturally.

After over a year and a half of dating, Simon's passion for Judy and interest in the relationship began to wane due to him feeling conflicted about how he felt about her. After several nights out with his buddies, a host of nostalgic feelings for his past single life began to cloud his judgment and make him question his love for her. Because Simon's inattention was palpable, eventually Judy communicated to him that she felt neglected and told Simon that she needed some time away from him.

It was difficult, but Judy knew better than to stay on a sinking ship. And to protect her heart, Judy did not contact Simon during their time apart as she knew that Simon, like all men, needed to be sure of what *he* really wanted and that he required both physical and emotional distance away from her love and tenderness to know for sure. Fortunately, her poise and **passive perseverance** proved irresistible, as after little over one month had passed, Simon came running back to her and begged her to never leave his side again.

Where a Woman's True Power Lies

I just gave you an example of two love-worthy ladies who responded very differently when faced with men who pulled away or lost interest. In that example, Judy was the one who eventually attracted the relationship she wanted because she didn't allow men to put her into "chase mode" whenever they pulled away emotionally or appeared to have lost interest in her.

Judy gets it. And the reason why she gets it is because she realizes one core thing about men, and it's this: **Men are the gatekeepers of commitment.** Whenever a guy is unsure about you, this is simply *his* decision to make. As a woman, your power lies in fully accepting that a man, even your man, requires the freedom to choose the woman he really wants to be with. If that woman happens to be you…great, but if that woman is not you, then so be it.

The less you attempt to control him or the situation, the more attractive you become to him. And by focusing on controlling the type of meaning you attach to such situations you end up having an immense power over your own emotions. This will keep you from chasing a guy who's pulling away from you or from becoming utterly distraught whenever a man acts ambivalent towards you.

At the end of the day, you are only in control of your own thoughts and behavior, nothing more, nothing less. While you can *influence* a man's behavior through gracious interaction with him, you cannot and should not desire to control his behavior. A woman's energy is best spent in the management of her deportment, so that no man, no matter how high-status, physically attractive, or charming, can rob her of her happiness and self-possession. If you can remain unmoved and unperturbed when a once seemingly passionate suitor withdraws emotionally, you will be surprised how fast his full attention falls back onto you once he realizes that:

1. He has little to no control over your sense of self-worth, and...

2. You have no intentions of controlling him either.

I think we can agree that having someone lead you on only to disappear out of your life is flagrantly disrespectful, regardless of whether it happens to a man or a woman. I think we can also agree that it would be best if people dated with a higher regard for the dignity of others, as putting a little more thoughtfulness and etiquette in dismissing a love interest we no longer desired would make the dating experience far more enjoyable for everyone on the whole.

However, while it's always fun to *wish* and *wonder* how things should be, you're going to have far more success with men and dating by accepting the way things actually are at the moment. *Wishing* men were different puts you in the position of the victim, and as is the nature of the victim, you are thus **powerless**. If you become a slave to your emotions and are unwilling or unable to change the way you handle and respond to a withdrawing man, then you will remain at the mercy of a man's desire or lack thereof. Never relinquish your power to a man by pursuing him when he pulls away or going out on a manhunt for him when he vanishes.

I know this might be hard to fathom, especially if men have mistreated you in the past, but make no mistake: The man who really wants to be with you will make this fact clear and consistent from the beginning. You won't have to second-guess yourself, constantly check in with your girlfriends to see what they think, or email your dating coach to gain some clarity on your situation. It will be embarrassingly obvious that he's into you.

As your relationship develops over time and your Mr. McDreamy's passion begins to naturally wane, don't rely on the words he uses to describe how he feels about you. You *must* pay attention to his actions, both their consistency and significance when it comes to being with you. You *must* honestly ask yourself: *"Does his actions display the love of a mature man who knows what he wants or do they display the fleeting fancies of a boy who doesn't know what he wants?"*

Remember, a man must be mature enough to recognize the difference between romantic love and unconditional love before he can give you the love and commitment you deserve. He must also be mature enough to accept the fact that while romantic love shrinks and grows, and comes and goes like the seasons; unconditional love can last for a lifetime and beyond.

You want to be with a man who is willing to offer you a wholehearted commitment to both you AND the relationship itself; the kind of man who is so fiercely protective of both your heart and your dignity that the importance he's placed on the integrity of the relationship is either equal to or greater than the importance you've placed on it. Believe me, when a man really wants you, where he doesn't want to be with anyone else and doesn't want anyone else to be with you, his commitment to the commitment itself will show it. Remember that.

By the way...

As a way of saying "thanks" for your purchase, I'm offering a free 10-lesson email course (and other assorted goodies) that are exclusive to my book readers. Each lesson reveals some of my best-kept dating secrets for cultivating **long-term attraction** with high-quality men.

You can access it at: http://www.brucebryans.com/ecourse/

In this free course, you will not only learn the most high-value dating behaviours that make men burn with desire and desperate to commit to a woman, but you'll also learn how to confidently interact with men so that you can get the guy you want, keep him interested, and quickly weed out time-wasters, players, and men who'll never commit.

In this knowledge-packed course, you'll discover:

- How to stand your ground and confidently communicate your boundaries in a way that INCREASES a man's attraction to you instead of turning him off.

- The one thing you absolutely MUST do when the man you love and want begins to pull away from you in a relationship.

- How to quickly hook Mr. Right from the first few dates by doing something MOST women are terrified of doing after meeting a great guy.

- What to do when a man says he "loves you" but he doesn't call you enough (or perhaps even at all).

- The #1 key to conquering the masculine heart and how to use this knowledge to cultivate DEEP feelings of love in a man. (Hint: This is the fastest way to tap into a man's emotional needs and make him see you as "Girlfriend Material.")

- A simple way to SKYROCKET your chances of meeting Mr. Right instead of desperately waiting for a "stroke of luck" to change your love life.

And much, much more…

Click the link below now if you're ready to join the thousands of other women who have used these attraction secrets to get more confidence, power, and results with men and dating.

Again, you can access it at:

http://www.brucebryans.com/ecourse/

See you on the inside,

Bruce

Before you go...

I just wanted to say "thank you" for purchasing my book.

I know you could have picked from dozens of books on understanding men, but you took a chance on my guide and for that I'm extremely grateful. So, thanks again for purchasing this book and reading all the way to the end.

Now, if you liked this book, **please take a minute or two to leave a review for it on Amazon so that other women just like you can find out more about it**. Your feedback is most appreciated as it helps me to continue writing books that get you results.

And "thank you" in advance for your review. I am eternally grateful.

Dating & Attraction Books by Bruce Bryans:

Below is a list of my books for women that you can find on Amazon.com. You can easily find them all here at: http://www.amazon.com/author/brucebryans

***

Texts So Good He Can't Ignore: Sassy Texting Secrets for Attracting High-Quality Men (and Keeping the One You Want)

In *Texts So Good He Can't Ignore*, you'll discover how to use texting to easily create attraction with your guy and finally get him OFF of his smartphone and ON more dates with you.

Never Chase Men Again: 38 Dating Secrets to Get the Guy, Keep Him Interested, and Avoid Dead-End Relationships

In *Never Chase Men Again*, you'll learn how to get the guy you want, train him to pursue you, and avoid dead-end or even "dead-on-arrival" relationships by being more assertive and communicating high-value to the men you date.

How To Get A Man Without Getting Played: 29 Dating Secrets to Catch Mr. Right, Set Your Standards, and Eliminate Time Wasters

In *How To Get A Man Without Getting Played*, you'll discover the beliefs, attitudes, dating rules, "love habits", and seduction secrets high-value women use to eliminate time wasters and find Mr. Right.

He's Not That Interested, He's Just Passing Time: 40 Unmistakable Behaviors of Men Who Avoid Commitment and Play Games with Women

In *He's Not That Interested, He's Just Passing Time*, you'll learn how to read a man's behavior to find out if he wants a relationship with you or if he's just leading you on and completely wasting your time.

Never Get Ghosted Again: 15 Reasons Why Men Lose Interest and How to Avoid Guys Who Can't Commit

In *Never Get Ghosted Again*, you'll discover the secret reasons why men lose interest, what causes men to fall in and out of love, and how to prevent *great* guys from disappearing on you.

The 7 Irresistible Qualities Men Want In A Woman: What High-Quality Men Secretly Look for When Choosing "The One"

In *The 7 Irresistible Qualities Men Want In A Woman*, you'll discover the feminine qualities that commitment ready, high-quality men look for when choosing a long-term mate.

Make Him BEG For Your Attention: 75 Communication Secrets for Captivating Men and Getting the Love and Commitment You Deserve

In *Make Him BEG For Your Attention*, you'll discover how to talk to a man so that he listens to you, opens up to you, and gives you what you want without a fuss.

Dating Deal Breakers That Drive Men Away: 12 Relationship Killers That Ruin Your Long-term Potential with High-Quality Men

In *Dating Deal Breakers That Drive Men Away*, you'll learn the most common dating red flags that high-quality men consider "deal-breakers", the kind of deal-breakers that compel them to stop pursuing a woman, ignore her texts (and phone calls), and eventually blow up a budding relationship.

Send Him A Signal: 61 Secrets for Indicating Interest and Attracting the Attention of Higher Quality Men

In *Send Him A Signal*, you'll learn the subtle signs of female interest that entices men to pursue a woman and also how to become more approachable to high-quality guys.

101 Things Your Dad Never Told You About Men: The Good, Bad, and Ugly Things Men Want and Think About Women and Relationships

In *101 Things Your Dad Never Told You About Men*, you'll learn what high-quality men want from women and what they think about love, sex, and romance. You'll learn how to seduce the man you want or captivate the man you love because you'll know exactly what makes him tick.

101 Reasons Why He Won't Commit To You: The Secret Fears, Doubts, and Insecurities That Prevent Most Men from Getting Married

In *101 Reasons Why He Won't Commit To You*, you'll learn the most common fears, doubts, and insecurities that paralyze men and prevent them from making the leap from boyfriend to husband.

About Bruce Bryans

Bruce Bryans is a successful author with a passion for research into the dating and mating rituals of men and women. He doesn't fashion himself as some all-knowing "relationship guru", but instead prefers to provide insightful information based on the social and biological factors that bring men and women together for love and romance. Bruce has written numerous books on topics including: masculinity, attraction, dating strategy, and gender dynamics within romantic relationships. Bruce's main aim is to provide easy-to-implement, practical information that helps men and women improve their dating market value and mating desirability to the opposite sex.

When he isn't tucked away in some corner writing a literary masterpiece (or so he thinks), Bruce spends most of his time engaged in manly hobbies, spending time with friends, or being a lovable nuisance to his wife and children.

You can learn more about his writings and receive updates (and future discounts) on his books by visiting his website at: www.BruceBryans.com

Share the Secrets

If you've been empowered, enlightened, or helped in any way by this book, please recommend it to your sisters, daughters, co-workers, and friends. If you're a blogger or fellow author, consider recommending it to your readers. And if you're a dating coach, therapist, counselor, etc., and you strongly believe that this book can help your clients, please consider recommending it to them or purchasing copies to give away as gifts.

I sincerely hope this book does wonders not only for your love life, but for the lives of the women you care about as well.

Here's to your success!

Bruce Bryans

Made in the USA
Monee, IL
01 June 2021